ARIZONA
H I G H W A Y S
THE LAW OF THE GUN

BY MARSHALL TRIMBLE

Book Editor:
BOB ALBANO

Marshall Trimble's roots reach deeply into American military and lawman history. His ancestors were officers in the Revolutionary Army and fought under Andy Jackson at the Battle of Horseshoe Bend and the Battle of New Orleans.

The author's great-great-grandfather, Moffett Trimble, was a Texas Ranger under the legendary Sam Walker during the Mexican War. His great-grandfather, Sam Walker Trimble, served in a Texas cavalry regiment during the Civil War and later fought with John Ford's Texas Rangers in the Indian Wars, taking part in the *Battle on the Frio,* in 1866. Sam Walker Trimble later was a peace officer, professional gambler, and stockman in Texas.

Music led Marshall Trimble into writing and teaching Western history. He bought a used Gibson guitar for $5 in 1957 and learned to play while listening to Elvis Presley, Buddy Holly and Johnny Cash records. A couple of years later he attended a Kingston Trio concert and became hooked on folk music. In 1963, he joined a folk singing group called the Gin Mill Three. The group cut four records and played Las Vegas, Reno, Lake Tahoe, and San Francisco. A promoter changed their name to the Prairie Boys, hoping it would present a cleaner image. The group broke up after two years when one member got drafted and another got married.

Trimble returned to music in 1971 with a folk duo called Donnery and Rudd. "I don't know whether I was Donnery or Rudd," Trimble says. "We took the name from the label on a bottle of Cutty Sark scotch."

While studying the origins of folk music, Trimble took an interest in the history of the American West. In 1972, he began teaching Arizona and Southwest history at Scottsdale Community College, and at the urging of his students, wrote *Arizona: A Panoramic History of a Frontier State.* The book, published by Doubleday, became a best seller. He has written 13 books on Arizona and the West. His credits include several articles for *Arizona Highways* and authorship along with two others of *Travel Arizona: The Back Roads,* published by *Arizona Highways.*

During the mid-70s Trimble began singing folk tunes again, with an emphasis on old cowboy songs and poetry. In 1988 he wrote and recorded *Legends in Levis,* a tribute to Old West cowboys. His poetry has been published in national magazines such as *The American Cowboy.*

Trimble combines musical talents with his knowledge of history and folklore to entertain audiences with songs, tales, and cowboy poetry. He has appeared on *Good Morning America*, *This Morning,* and has opened concerts for such acts as Waylon Jennings, the Oak Ridge Boys, and Jerry Lee Lewis.

The Arizona Historical Foundation said of Marshall Trimble: "Warm, witty, intelligent and always entertaining. … Marshall's homespun wit and unassuming demeanor often serve as a smoke screen to his incisive talents in scholarly arenas."

See page 192 for other comments about Trimble.

This book is dedicated to the men and women who enforce the law today and to the memory of the peace officers of yesteryear.

It took a brave, hard breed of men to tangle with the depraved border marauders who often killed needlessly and without remorse. Many lawmen were family men working for little pay. They endured hardships, hunger and sometimes they died in the line of duty, leaving their families destitute. Most served because it was the right thing to do, feeling a sense of duty to build a safer place for their children to grow up.

Law officers today have that same spirit.

Design: MARY WINKELMAN VELGOS
Front cover art: JUDY MILLER
Back cover art: KEVIN KIBSEY
Photographic enhancement: VICKY SNOW
Copy Editor: CHARLES BURKHART

Photographs furnished by the Department of Southwest Studies,
Maricopa Community Colleges.

The front cover montage depicts, from upper left, Sheriff George Ruffner,
Pancho Villa, Sheriff Buckey O'Neill (second from right) and members of his
Canyon Diablo posse, and the Colt Peacemaker.

Prepared by the Book Division of *Arizona Highways*® magazine, a monthly
publication of the Arizona Department of Transportation.

Publisher — Nina M. La France
Managing Editor — Bob Albano
Associate Editor — Robert J. Farrell
Art Director — Mary Winkelman Velgos
Production Director — Cindy Mackey

Printed in the United States
Library of Congress Catalog Number 97-72795
ISBN 0-916179-69-9

C O N T E N T S

The Old West Mystique: When the Law of the Gun Ruled

A MERICA'S FASCINATION WITH THE OLD WEST BEGAN IN the early 1870s with magazines such as *Police Gazette*, *Harper's*, and *Frank Leslie's Weekly*. The pink-colored *Gazette* was the first to mold the image; the latter two were less garish but perhaps more factual. All three published stories of the frontier that were read in cow camps, bordellos, saloons, and barber shops.

Dime novels created larger-than-life heroes such as "Deadwood Dick" and "Arizona Joe." Women were romanticized in the adventures of "Hurricane Nell," "Bess the Trapper," and "Mountain Kate." These novels also featured real-life figures such as Calamity Jane, Wild Bill Hickok, and Jesse James, who always appeared as swashbucklers.

More than a few cowboys, gunfighters, and outlaws modeled their own characters on dime novel heroes. Teddy Roosevelt, when he was ranching in the Dakotas, once helped capture some outlaws. Inside the desperados' saddlebags were pulp Westerns. Famed scout Kit Carson was a modest, unassuming man not given to boasting, but when he saw a magazine cover showing him fighting Indians with one arm and holding a helpless maiden with the other, he remarked: "I ain't got no recollection of it."

The Old West mystique has captured the imagination of people worldwide. From Scandinavia through

A TYPICAL SALOON IN THE OLD WEST

western Europe to the Mediterranean, the fascination with America's frontier has spawned clubs of wannabe cowboys and gunfighters. Some even re-enact events such as the gunfight at O.K. Corral.

In the 1870s, German writer Karl May wrote thrillers about an American West he had never seen. May's books have sold more than 45 million copies in Germany alone.

The Old West was one of a kind! Other countries, such as Australia and Africa, had raw, untamed frontiers, but none possessed the combination of size and beauty that made the Old West special. The West offered, as writer Bret Harte said: "A fresh deal all around."

It challenged men and women to come out and make a life. The legions of stalwarts included mountain men, trailblazers, Indians, miners, prospectors, preachers, teachers, freighters, soldiers, railroaders, merchants, lumberjacks, steamboat pilots, farmers, cattlemen and cowhands, and an intrepid breed known as gunfighters.

Much of the Old West mystique centers on the men who used guns to uphold or break the law.

Arizona was the last sanctuary for outlaws in the Old West. Law and order came earlier to places like Texas, New Mexico, Montana, and Wyoming, driving the lawless elements to wilder refuges. In Arizona, towns were few and far between, there hardly were any roads, and endless stretches of unpopulated country provided refuge for desperados on the run. More than 300 miles along the unguarded Mexican border consisted of an awesome land of jagged, brawny mountains; twisting, steep-sided canyons; and hot, searing deserts sprawling beneath a persistent sun. It was a good place to grow rattlesnakes, Gila monsters, and scorpions, and it was a good place to harbor desperate men.

Arizona's fabulously rich gold, silver, and copper strikes attracted outlaws looking for easy money. Stagecoaches hauling payroll and bullion to and from the mines had to pass through narrow, treacherous canyons. The steam locomotives pulling Wells Fargo express cars were slowed to a crawl on the long grades. Both were vulnerable to the gangs of desperados who preyed upon them. Gangs of rustlers brazenly stole cattle from honest ranchers in broad daylight, or made moonlight raids into Mexico. They sold stolen cattle at bargain prices to citizens who were more interested in turning profits than checking to see if the goods were stolen.

Lawmen were at a distinct disadvantage to apprehend these miscreants. County and state borders limited the pursuit of outlaws.

Arizona lawmen would ride into the back country in

pursuit of outlaws and find the local citizens unwilling to cooperate. Locals knew the law would only be around for a few days and the outlaws would make any honest citizen pay dearly for any assistance given to the officers.

At times they had to ride into the lair of the outlaw where they were at a disadvantage against desperate men who knew the lay of the land much better than they did. They had to be every bit as tough as the men they pursued and in the end Arizona's peace officers were usually up to the task.

It wasn't until 1901, when the Arizona Rangers were organized that non-federal lawmen could pursue outlaws across county lines. An informal arrangement with the Mexican *Rurales* enabled the Rangers to slip across the border to apprehend fugitives. Sometimes the Mexicans just nabbed the scoundrel and delivered him to a Ranger waiting at the border.

Bringing law and order to Arizona was a long and difficult task. At the beginning of the 20th century trains were still being robbed and large outlaw gangs still rode the rugged mountains of eastern Arizona. The citizens were clamoring for statehood but the politicians in Washington were skeptical. Hair-raising tales of raiding Apaches, feuds, train robberies, and gangs of cattle rustlers had branded Arizona as a place unfit for statehood because it still was ruled by the law of the gun.

On the following pages are chapters focusing on facts and fantasies of Western gunfighters, the guns they used, and biographical sketches of seven figures whose exploits blazed across Arizona.

CHAPTER ONE

The Western Gunfighter: Facts and Fantasies

———◆◆◆———

T HE GUNFIGHTER WAS THE EMBODIMENT OF AN AMERICAN legend. They were called hellers, shooters, shootists, civilizers, gunmen, gunslingers, bravos, mankillers, pistoleers, and pistoleros.

The word gunfighter can be traced to 1874, but it did not become popular until the early part of the 20th century, when gunfighters were fading from reality into myth.

Most gunfighters were flamboyant, attracting women and inspiring admiration or provoking fear in men. Contrary to myth, not all were cowboys. Many preferred to dress in the fashion of the day, earning their livings as peace officers or professional gamblers.

Many of the men who survived the horrors of the Civil War were haunted by the specter of imminent death. Some migrated to the untamed West, but couldn't turn off the violence. For them, the war would never end. Also, bad blood between ex-Union and ex-Confederate soldiers spilled over into the West. Indeed, many of the shootings in the rough cow town saloons were rooted in the Civil War.

Drinking and gambling fueled the rowdy nature of frontier towns. Frontier people had their own rules of conduct, and most had to fend for themselves. Survival depended on the ability to handle a gun.

City fathers often hired people known for their skill with a gun to tame towns. Some were lawful; others were bad; most were somewhere in between. Some, like "Bear River Tom" Smith, were the stuff of dime-novel heroes. Others, like Henry Plummer, were as hard-bitten and intractable as the men they were hired to corral.

BILL TILGHMAN

Smith enforced the law in Abilene, Kansas. Without a gun, he faced many dangerous adversaries. On November 2, 1870, he was murdered with an ax while attempting to make an arrest.

Plummer, an outlaw who became a lawman to cover his illicit activities, had murdered several men in California by the time he arrived in Montana in 1862. He became city marshal of the mining boom town Virginia City. At the same time he led a gang of desperados known as the Innocents. Vigilantes finally caught up with the gang and about 20 Innocents, including Plummer, were shot or hanged. Ironically, the lawman was hanged on his own gallows.

Bill Tilghman may have been the West's greatest peace officer. He, along with lawmen Heck Thomas and Chris Madsen, were known as the Guardsmen. They played a large part in ridding Oklahoma of outlaw gangs around the turn of the century.

As a youth, Tilghman was arrested twice for theft,

but marriage and family turned his life around. As a lawman, he helped round up the Dalton, Starr, Jennings, and Doolin gangs. In 1915, after a long and distinguished career, he went to Hollywood to be technical advisor on a movie, *The Passing of the Oklahoma Outlaws*.

Tilghman was called out of retirement in the 1920s to tame the oil boom town of Cromwell, Oklahoma. There, on the evening of October 26, 1926, the 70-year-old lawman was shot to death.

Jim Roberts had a big role in Arizona's Pleasant Valley War in the late 1880s. He was indicted in that feud, but the murder charge was dismissed. Later he became one of Arizona's top peace officers. In 1928, when he was nearly 70 years old, Roberts happened on the scene in Clarkdale as two bank robbers were speeding away in an automobile. One fired a shot at the old gunfighter. Roberts drew his revolver and shot the driver in the head.

Some gunfighters — Wyatt Earp among them — were entrepreneurs who speculated on mining and real estate schemes. Often, they supplemented their income as professional gamblers, sometimes using a badge to back their play. Others, like the hard-drinking ex-Texas Ranger Bass Outlaw (his real name), were psychopathic killers battling their personal demons.

In Outlaw's case, it was an inferiority complex. He stood only a little over 5 feet tall but was extremely violent when provoked. During one of his rampages in an El Paso bordello he was shot and killed by lawman John Selman, who once had been an outlaw.

Gunfighters were a product of their violent times. Noted gunfighter authority Joseph Rosa wrote:

"(They were) part man, part myth, based on the exploits of a breed of men spawned in the war with Mexico in 1846. In adolescence they witnessed the California Gold Rush of 1849, the Kansas-Missouri border wars of the 1850s, and during the Civil War reached maturity fighting as guerrillas on both sides. Adult life was spent in the post-war cattle, rail and mining boom towns, and during this turbulent period they came into their own."

Their common bond was the ability to kill. Wild Bill Hickok spoke for the breed when he said: "As to killing, I never think much about it. I don't believe in ghosts, and I don't keep the lights burning all night to keep them away. That's because I'm not a murderer. It is the other man or me in a fight, and I don't stop to think: is it a sin to do this thing? And after it's over, what's the use of disturbing the mind?"

One product of the post-Civil War violence in Texas was called the "deadliest killer of 'em all." He was John Wesley Hardin and, it was said, he gunned down 20 to 40 men. Hardin, the son of a Methodist circuit rider and an ex-school teacher, believed all his victims "needed killin'."

Texas Rangers finally caught up with Hardin and he spent 15 years in prison, where he studied law. Two years before his release, his wife, Jane, died.

After his release in 1894, Hardin married 14-year-old Callie Lewis after winning her from her father in a poker game. She left him on their wedding day. Hardin headed for El Paso, where he opened a law practice and met a buxom ex-prostitute named Beulah Morose. Beulah's husband, Martin, was a cattle rustler and at the time was hiding across the Rio Grande at Juarez.

JEFF MILTON AND GEORGE SCARBOROUGH

The affair began when Beulah asked Hardin to represent her husband. Beulah traded her professional services for Hardin's.

Hardin learned that the couple had stashed a large sum of money. Wanting it, and Beulah, Hardin conspired to have Martin killed.

According to a story told later, El Paso Police Chief Jeff Milton, George Scarborough, and Frank Mahon, all lawmen of renown, would each get $1,000 to kill the outlaw. The fourth man in the purported scheme was old John Selman, Sr., an El Paso constable. Like Hardin, he was a fearless gunfighter who had worked on both sides of the law, but now he was half-blind and crippled by Mexican black smallpox.

On June 29, 1894, the four men lured Morose to the border under the pretense of meeting Beulah, then gunned him down with shotguns, rifles, and pistols. The citizens of El Paso were outraged, saying that even an outlaw deserved better. But the shooters were acquitted. It was said that Hardin failed to divide the money with them.

A few weeks after the killing of Martin Morose, John Selman, Jr. arrested Beulah for drunkenness. Hardin went into a rage, threatening to kill both Selmans. By this time Hardin and Beulah were drinking hard and fighting often. Once, he forced her to write a note saying she was committing suicide. She wrote the note, but before he could kill her, Hardin passed out on the bed. She called the police and had him arrested. Another time she decided to move to Arizona, but on the way had a premonition of his death and returned to El Paso. Their compatibility didn't get any better, however, and soon she left for good.

Hardin seemed to be haunted by the killing of Morose and once threatened to clear his conscience by telling all.

On the evening of April 19, 1895, old John Selman walked into the Acme Saloon where Hardin was gambling with Henry Brown, a local grocer.

"You have four sixes to beat," Hardin told Brown. Just then, a bullet slammed into the back of Hardin's head and came out his left eye. As Hardin slumped to the floor, Selman walked over and shot him twice more.

The body was left lying on the barroom floor for two hours so citizens could parade by and have a last look at the infamous John Wesley Hardin.

The trial of John Selman ended in a hung jury. Before he could be tried again, Selman was killed by George Scarborough. Four years to the day after he killed Selman, Scarborough was killed by New Mexico train robbers.

At Selman's trial, the coroner claimed the bullet entered the back of Hardin's head, but Selman insisted the bullet entered through the left eye and exited the back of his head. Was it murder or self-defense? When expert witness George Higgins was asked about the wound he replied, "If John Wesley Hardin was shot in the front, it was excellent marksmanship. If he was shot in the back, it was excellent judgment."

JOHN WESLEY HARDIN

Myths surrounding the deeds of gunfighters abound.

One of them insists that Jesse James stole from the rich and gave to the poor. If he stole from the rich, it was because there was no profit in stealing from the poor.

According to myth, Wild Bill Hickok slew 30 terrorists in one fight. Actually he killed only one in that fight, an unarmed farmer named David McCanles. Throughout his career, Hickok probably killed only seven or eight men.

Henry McCarty — a.k.a. William Antrim, a.k.a. William Bonney, a.k.a. Billy the Kid — was supposed to have killed 21 men before Sheriff Pat Garrett gunned him down in 1881 at Fort Sumner, New Mexico. A more accurate number of Billy's victims is four.

It was said that Bat Masterson killed 31 bad guys before heading east to become a sports writer. Actually, the sheriff of Ford County, Kansas, killed one man and possibly wounded a woman. Years later, while working as a sports writer in New York City, Bat obliged his many admirers by presenting each his "personal six-shooter." He would go to a local gun store, purchase a Peacemaker, and carve several notches on the handle.

Much of the violent image of the West was due to pulp Westerns published by Beadle and Adams.

In 1869, Edward Z. C. Judson, writing under the name Ned Buntline, went West to persuade Major Frank North to appear in a Wild West show. North, a legitimate Western hero, was leader of the Pawnee Scouts. He was no fan of Buntline's pulp novels and turned him down cold.

Undaunted, Buntline found a young man named Bill Cody sleeping under a wagon. They struck up a friendship, and Ned returned to the East where he cranked out a series of dime novels heralding the adventures of Frank North but using Cody's name. The legend of Bill Cody or "Buffalo Bill" was born. Then Buntline persuaded Cody to participate in a stage play. Soon afterward, Cody formed his own Wild West show.

In 1887, dime novelists introduced Buck Taylor as the "King of the Cowboys." He and others like him became the gunfighter heroes of folklore.

In 1903, Owen Wister wrote the prototype of tight-lipped heroes, *The Virginian*. That same year Edwin S. Porter filmed *The Great Train Robbery*, the first motion picture with a story line, in the "wilds" of New Jersey. Audiences demanded more. At the same time, real outlaws were robbing trains out West. Two desperados, Butch Cassidy and the Sundance Kid, reputedly visited a movie theater in New York City and saw themselves portrayed on the screen robbing a train and shooting passengers indiscriminately. That must have been a particular shock to Butch, since he had never shot anybody. They also saw themselves gunned down by a posse at the movie's end.

Shoot-outs at high noon, the trademark of Western movies, were rare in the Old West. Rosa, the gunfighter authority, wrote that between the Civil War and the turn of the century, there were only 39 so-called "classic" gun-fights.

A classic man-to-man gunfight in the street did occur on July 21, 1865. Wild Bill Hickok and an Arkansas gambler named Dave Tutt faced off in the town square in Springfield, Missouri. They were rivals for the affections of a lady named Susanna Moore, and that was a probable cause for the shoot-out.

Trouble began one night when the two were playing cards. Hickok ran out of money and put his gold watch on the table as collateral. He lost and went for money to retrieve his watch. When he returned, Tutt refused to relinquish it. Exchanging threats, they agreed to meet the next day and settle the matter with six-guns.

The next evening around 6 o'clock the two faced off in the town square before a large crowd. Tutt tauntingly displayed the pocket watch belonging to Hickok. Both men began advancing, and, at about 75 yards, they started firing. Tutt missed. Wild Bill, laying his gun barrel across his left forearm, took aim and put a bullet through Tutt's heart.

In the real West, if a man were gunning for another, he would avoid a showdown and use every advantage possible, even if it meant sneaking up and shooting his foe in the back. To square off and tell the other man to "draw" always gave the other guy a split-second edge.

Usually, if one or the other didn't have the edge, the fight never got past the talking. "Code duello" was for pulp

Westerns and motion pictures. Back shooting might have been frowned upon in the Code of the West, but it certainly wasn't unusual. Getting the drop on an adversary — and staying alive —were all that really counted.

One notorious outlaw who tried to sneak up on a lawman made a fatal error. Early one morning in Willcox in 1908, Bill Downing was bellied up to the bar at the Free and Easy Saloon when he heard Arizona Ranger Billy Speed calling for his arrest from out in the street. Downing slipped out the back door hoping to get the drop on the Ranger. He failed to notice that some good citizen had pilfered the pistol from his holster. The Ranger anticipated Downing's move, and the two met coming around the corner. Downing reached for his pistol and inspired an axiom for those who choose to live by the gun: Don't go for your gun unless you're sure it's there. Henceforth, he was known as the late Bill Downing.

Deception was also part of winning the fight. Bill Mulvey got the drop on Wild Bill Hickok one day in Hays City. Hickok looked over Mulvey's shoulder and shouted, "Don't shoot him boys, he's drunk and doesn't know what he's doin'." Mulvey was distracted just long enough for the marshal to draw his pistol and dispatch him.

Hickok probably was the greatest shootist of them all. His skill as a marksman with a six-gun, even considering embellishments, isn't challenged. But the number of men he is supposed to have gunned down has been exaggerated. Not counting the wars, the so-called "Prince of Pistoleers" killed only seven or eight men in gunfights. Myth makers, including Hickok, tallied that number up to 100.

During his checkered career, Hickok was a Union spy

and scout for the Army against the Indians. He hunted on the Plains with the royal Russian family and toured with Buffalo Bill's Wild West Show. He battled a wild bear, had numerous gunfights with rough and tumble cowboys up the trail from Texas, and engaged in an uneven fight with three Nebraska farmers.

Hickok stood over six feet tall, was broad-shouldered, with blond hair that reached to his shoulders. He had an aquiline nose and high-pitched voice.

His dress set the style for gunfighters of his era. Wild Bill favored long-tailed frock coats, fancy vests, and ruffled shirts. His effeminate mannerisms belied the fact that he spent a lot of time in fancy ladies' bedrooms. Most of his shooting scrapes can be traced to love triangles. When he wasn't taming Hays City or Abilene, Marshal Hickok usually could be found in one of the local brothels.

Wild Bill's other hobby was gambling, although his hand at cards wasn't nearly as skillful as his prowess with a six-gun.

Like many larger-than-life Western figures, Hickok was a walking contradiction. He was one of the greatest shooters of his time and a fearless lawman.

Hickok feared assassination by glory hunters. He spread newspapers on his bedroom floor to make noise in case someone tried to sneak up on him while he was sleeping. He avoided bright lights and dark alleys. He would walk into a barroom through a side or back door, or if he came in through the front he would quickly step to one side before he could be "framed" in the doorway. While playing poker, he would sit with his back to the wall. If Wild Bill seemed paranoid, it was with good reason. He had made many enemies, especially among the Texas drovers.

Wild Bill's last gunfight occurred on October 5, 1871, in Abilene, Kansas, about six months after he was appointed city marshal. It was a tough job, keeping the boisterous cowboys in line while allowing them to spend all their money in town.

The Bull's Head Saloon, owned by Texans Ben Thompson and Phil Coe, was the town's most raucous joint. Citizens protested when the proprietors displayed a

JAMES BUTLER HICKOK: "WILD BILL"

painting of a bull with a particular part of its anatomy displayed prominently. Hickok, with a shotgun resting in the crook of his arm, presided while the bull's genitals were eradicated with a paint brush. This heightened animosity between Hickok and the two saloonkeepers.

The rival factions snarled at each other but did not engage in gunplay.

Eventually, Thompson returned to Texas and Coe sold his interest in the saloon but remained as a professional gambler. Troubles might have ended except for a saloon girl named Jesse Hazel, who was being courted by both Hickok and Coe. Talk around town was it wouldn't take much for the two to have a shoot-out.

On the night of October 5, a bunch of cowboys were in town celebrating the end of the trail-driving season. Hickok was on patrol, assisted by policeman Mike Williams.

Coe and some friends also were celebrating, and as they approached the Alamo Saloon, a dog growled at him. Coe shot at the dog and missed. Hickok arrived, demanding to know who had fired the shot. When Coe confessed, Hickok shot him in the stomach. Coe returned the fire, putting two bullets through Wild Bill's frock coat.

About that time, Williams rushed to the scene, and Hickok, believing one of Coe's friends was trying to bushwhack him, spun around and fired, mortally wounding his young assistant. A tearful Wild Bill carried him into the Alamo. Coe lived for three days in pain before dying.

After the shooting, Hickok went on a rampage, tearing up saloons, shooting out lights, and challenging the Texas cowboys to fight or get out of town. Nobody took up the challenge. He was relieved of his duties on December 13, 1871. After that, he never again would wear a lawman's badge.

By then, Hickok had survived seven gunfights and several skirmishes with ex-Confederates and Indians, but he who lives by the gun dies by the gun. On August 2, 1876, in Deadwood, South Dakota, he was shot in the back of the head by a drifter named Jack McCall. Wild Bill had been having a bad day at poker when the fatal shot rang out. He slumped to the floor still clutching his cards, two aces and two eights, a hand that is still known as the "dead man's hand."

Wild Bill's bad luck ran deep that day. Later, it was found that the only round in McCall's six-shooter that was not defective was the one that got Hickok.

No legend fits the Robin Hood image better than that of Jesse James, but, in reality, his life bore little resemblance to the legend. He was the product of an era that spawned a breed that couldn't, or wouldn't, return to the normal life after the Civil War.

Jesse was born on September 5, 1847, in Clay County, Missouri, the son of a Baptist minister. Although he was four years younger than his brother Frank, Jesse was the natural leader of the pair. His father, Robert, joined the California gold rush and died of a fever in California, leaving his wife Zerelda to raise the boys. After a marriage that ended in divorce, she eventually married Reuben Samuel, a medical doctor and a farmer.

When war came, Frank went off to fight with William Quantrill's Raiders. Union soldiers came to the family farm seeking Frank. They tortured Dr. Samuel and locked up 16-year-old Jesse, but neither talked. Soon afterward, Jesse joined the rebels and rode with Quantrill's irregulars.

He also rode with "Bloody Bill" Anderson, a rogue, who tied his victims' scalps to his bridle. It was with him that young Jesse witnessed and participated in some of the horrors of guerrilla warfare.

On September 27, 1864, during a looting raid at Centralia, Missouri, Jesse, "Bloody Bill," and 30 guerrillas killed 25 unarmed Union soldiers. A year earlier, Frank James and Cole Younger had ridden with Anderson on the infamous raid of Lawrence, Kansas. That day, women and children were forced to watch while 150 unarmed men and boys were slaughtered.

The James boys' first bank robbery came nearly a year after the war ended. They took $60,000 from the Clay County Savings Bank on February 13, 1866. It was the first daylight bank robbery in America during peacetime.

Frank and Jesse had begun a career that would last

**JAMES AND YOUNGER BROTHERS:
FROM LEFT, COLE YOUNGER, JESSE JAMES,
BOB YOUNGER, AND FRANK JAMES**

about 15 years. They were joined in these escapades by their neighbors, Cole, Bob, John, and Jim Younger.

Banks and trains became their favorite targets, and no outlaws robbed with more daring. The banks and railroads hired the Pinkerton Detective Agency to hunt them down. Allan Pinkerton's detectives were so dogged in their pursuit of criminals that outlaws dubbed him "The Eye," a name suggested by the company logo. Later, this would give rise to the term "private eye."

Frank and Jesse James had a large following of local supporters, mostly Confederate sympathizers, who despised railroad companies and banks. Lawmen could expect little cooperation from them. It became customary after a robbery for Jesse to write an indignant letter to the local newspaper disclaiming any part in the crime. Sometimes the letter would be delivered by Jesse's mother. Some Missouri newspaper editors were staunch Confederate sympathizers and wrote editorials portraying Frank and Jesse as heroes persecuted because of their activities in the war.

Jesse liked to do things with flair. Once, while recovering from a gunshot wound, he and the doctor who patched him up sat and dined at a local hotel with Pinkerton agents who were hunting for him. Another time he visited with a detective who was pursuing him and a few days later, sent the man a postcard saying he had met Jesse James.

In 1874, Jesse married Zee Mimms, his lifelong sweetheart and first cousin. They had two children, but despite settling into family life, he continued to plan robberies and lead the gang. During this time Jesse regularly attended church.

On January 26, 1875, the Samuel family was again punished for the actions of the brothers. Pinkerton agents and a local posse surrounded the family's house. A bomb was hurled into the house, killing the Jameses' 9-year-old half-brother, Archie, and causing an injury that resulted in the amputation of their mother's hand. This act turned out to be a public relations disaster for the Pinkerton Agency, which claimed that the bomb incident was an accident.

An attempted bank robbery in Northfield, Minnesota, turned out to be a nightmare for the James gang. On September 7, 1876, the outlaws rode into Northfield, shouting and shooting. Cole Younger, pistols in both hands, shot at anything that moved. Jesse, Frank, and Charlie Pitts ran inside the bank. As Jesse stepped inside the vault, cashier Dick Heywood tried to slam the vault door on him. Before he could succeed, Pitts slapped his pistol barrel into the man's head, knocking him senseless. Teller A. E. Bunker was so frightened as he ran from the bank that he went through the closed front door. Pitts shot the running man in the shoulder.

Citizens reacted quickly, grabbing guns from two mercantile stores and firing on the outlaws. A young medical student drew a bead on one outlaw, Clell Miller, and dropped him with one shot. Years later the shooter displayed Miller's skeleton in his medical office.

Cole Younger took a bullet in the shoulder. He ran into the bank shouting, "Let's get out of here! They're killing us." Frank and Jesse grabbed only some change even though loot was inside the unlocked vault. On the way out, Jesse shot and killed a teller. As they ran from the bank, the outlaws were met with a barrage of gunfire.

In the street, Bob Younger's horse was shot from under him, and a bullet shattered his elbow. He took cover under a stairway. Bill Chadwell was shot and fell dead in the street. Jim Younger was hit in both shoulders, and a part of his jaw was blown away. Frank and Jesse suffered minor wounds from shotgun pellets. Only Charlie Pitts came through unscathed.

The bandits jumped on horses and made a break through the gunfire. Wounded and without a horse, Bob Younger called, "Don't leave me." Cole rode back through the fusillade and pulled his brother onto the saddle. What was left of the gang rode out of Northfield with a thousand-man posse in pursuit. Frank and Jesse were mounted on stolen plow horses. One was blind in one eye, the other was blind in both eyes.

During the flight, Frank and Jesse decided to go it alone. It was claimed later that Jesse wanted to shoot the wounded Bob Younger because he was slowing them down. Cole and Jim Younger refused to leave their brother behind. Charlie Pitts chose to stay with the Youngers. It was a fatal decision on his part.

Two weeks after the robbery, a posse closed in on Pitts and the Younger brothers. Pitts went down in a hail of gunfire. When the Younger brothers finally surrendered, Cole had 11 gunshot wounds, Bob had several minor wounds and a shattered elbow and Jim was full of buckshot in addition to the wounds he had suffered at the bank.

Frank and Jesse managed to shoot their way out of a trap near Lake Crystal, but both were gunshot in a freak occurrence. They were riding double when a bullet went through the horse, through Frank's knee, and lodged in Jesse's thigh.

Of the eight desperados who rode into Northfield, only Frank and Jesse escaped. In about 20 minutes poorly armed townsfolk had routed America's most celebrated gang of outlaws. Although Frank and Jesse recruited new members, their days as desperados were about over.

Jesse and his family were living under the alias "Howard" in St. Joseph, Missouri, when he was killed on April 3, 1882. Bob Ford, a gang member, shot him in the back. Ford did it for money. For his deed, the "dirty little coward, who shot Mr. Howard and laid poor Jesse in his grave," received $600. The rest of the $10,000 reward was divided among other "deserving parties," including Governor Thomas T. Crittenden.

Ten years later Bob Ford would be shot to death by a man named Ed O'Kelly, who wanted to be known as the "man who killed the man who killed Jesse James."

After Jesse's death, his guns, a Colt .45 and a Smith and Wesson Schofield .45, were auctioned off for $15.

Frank James managed to escape jail and eventually was pardoned. After Cole Younger was released from prison in 1901, the two, with limited success, went into show business with a Wild West show. Later, Cole went on the lecture circuit offering penitent themes such as "What Life Has Taught Me."

Frank died in 1915 at the family farm. His last years were spent giving tours of the place for four bits.

Earlier, Jesse's mother conducted the tours. The tour included an unrehearsed melodrama in which Zerelda alternately wept, then damned everything from Bob Ford to the Pinkertons to the unfair persecution of her sons. She supplemented her income by selling pebbles from Jesse's grave for a quarter each. Periodically, she replaced her supply from a nearby creek bed. Zerelda was an entrepreneur. She bought old pistols by the dozen and sold them to tourists as "the one Jesse carried."

After the Younger brothers' Aunt Adeline married Lewis Dalton, they became the parents of the next generation of outlaws, Bill, Bob, Grattan, and Emmett. Their reign of terror lasted about 18 months. Bob Dalton was the leader of the outfit. Other members included George "Bitter Creek" Newcomb, "Black Face" Charley Bryant, Bill Powers, Dick Broadwell, and Bill Doolin.

The gang was responsible for several train robberies, but the Daltons' ambition was to do something the

James-Younger gang had never done — rob two banks simultaneously in the same town.

The Daltons tried it in their hometown of Coffeyville, Kansas. They rode into town the morning of October 5, 1892.

There had been rumors of trouble, and Coffeyville was an armed camp. The Daltons should have been suspicious when they saw that the hitching rail in front of the bank had been removed.

Bob and Emmett entered the First National Bank, threw grain sacks at the tellers, and told them to fill 'em up. The tellers protested that the vault had a timer and could not be opened. Bob convinced them it would open, and it did. The sacks were filled with $21,000 in greenbacks. Bob and Emmett had done their part and they were ready to ride.

But things didn't go so smoothly for the others. Slow-witted Grat Dalton entered the Condon Bank with Bill Powers and Dick Broadwell. They covered the employees with Winchesters. "Open up the safe and open it quick," Grat ordered, tossing a grain sack on the floor.

"It's a time lock. Won't open until 9:45," responded cashier Charley Ball.

Grat hesitated, then said, "That is only three minutes … I will wait."

Soon, the citizens of the town began to pour heavy gunfire into the bank. Bill Powers and Dick Broadwell returned the fire. Grat asked a teller where the back door was. The teller said there wasn't one, and Grat believed him. Then the three gunmen grabbed what little cash they could carry, about $1,500, and started out the front door.

The delay had been crucial, giving citizens time to converge on the scene. Powers was hit and went down as he tried to mount his horse. Then Broadwell was hit. He climbed on his horse and bled to death as he rode out of town. Grat was hit a couple of times as he headed into what became known as "Death Alley." That episode was three minutes of hell.

Bob and Emmett came to help, but all were pinned down by heavy gunfire. Bob took a bullet in the chest, slumping to the ground, dazed. Then, another bullet struck him. Grat was wandering in a daze when he took a fatal shot in the neck.

Emmett, still clutching the grain sack containing $21,000, could have ridden away. But he turned and rode back into the gunfire to get his brother. He reached down to assist Bob into the saddle.

"Don't mind me, Emmett, I'm done for," he said. "Don't surrender; die game!"

At that moment a shotgun roared and Emmett, the youngest brother, tumbled from the saddle. Someone shouted, "They're all down." And the shooting ended.

Four outlaws and four townsmen died that day. The bodies of Bob, Grat, Broadwell, and Powers were stretched out for the photographer. Souvenir hunters took what they could from the bodies.

Nearly all the loot was recovered. When the books were checked, $20 was listed as missing from the Condon Bank. The First National Bank showed a surplus of $1.98.

Later Emmett Dalton would say, "I have dwelt on (Charley) Ball's behavior. His was the decisive act in Coffeyville that day. His shifty falsehood about the vault — which all the time was open to any hand — was to save his bank $18,000. It was also the cause of death of eight men within the next five minutes."

Although Bob Dalton was adept at planning and executing robberies, a lot of credit went to a pretty lady named Eugenia Moore. She acted as advance agent for the Daltons. Nobody expected a woman to be part of an outlaw gang, so she could do her work without arousing suspicion. Unfortunately for the Daltons, Eugenia died of cancer before the Coffeyville raid.

Fate was kind to Bill Doolin that day. His horse pulled up lame and he had to turn back. Later Doolin would form his own gang and would meet the same fatal end.

Emmett Dalton recovered and, after serving nearly 15 years in prison, married his old sweetheart, Julia Johnson. He went to Hollywood and gave advice on how to make Westerns. Like Cole Younger and Frank James, Emmett also lectured on the evils of a life of crime.

Another enigmatic outlaw shrouded in myth is Henry McCarty ... William Antrim ... William Bonney. He used all three, but was best known as Billy the Kid. Actually, during his heyday he was known simply as Kid.

Billy was born in New York City in 1859, one of two sons of Irish immigrants, Patrick and Catherine McCarty. After his father died the family moved to New Mexico where, in 1873, his mother married William Antrim. The family settled in Silver City where Billy's mother died the following year.

Billy's first criminal act was a paltry affair. He was caught stealing clothes from a Chinese laundry. He was arrested and jailed but escaped by climbing out the chimney. He fled to Arizona, where he joined a gang of rustlers and quickly gained a reputation among local lawmen as an escape artist.

At Fort Grant, Billy killed a barroom bully named Windy Cahill. The burly blacksmith slapped Billy around and generally abused him in front of the saloon crowd. One day he called Billy a pimp. Billy called him a son-of-a-bitch, and the two got into a fight. Billy pulled his pistol and shot the larger man in the belly. He probably would have gotten off with self-defense, but Billy decided to run.

Charged with murder, Billy headed back to New Mexico. There he went to work at the ranch of an Englishman named John Tunstall. Soon Billy was drawn into a feud that would make him a legend. The feud became known as the Lincoln County War.

On one side of this banking and mercantile feud was Lawrence G. Murphy and Jimmy Dolan. They had some high-ranking politicians in their pockets, including U.S. Attorney Thomas Catron and Sheriff William Brady. They also had the backing of the Santa Fe Ring, a group of crooked politicians who controlled New Mexico politics.

The opposing faction included Tunstall, rancher John Chisum, whose cattle were being stolen by the Murphy-Dolan crowd, and a lawyer named Alexander McSween.

In 1877, Tunstall and McSween opened a bank and mercantile store in Lincoln, going into competition with Murphy and Dolan. The new operation immediately began taking away business, and Murphy and Dolan coerced Sheriff Brady into filing trumped-up charges against Tunstall. A "posse" then murdered Tunstall in cold blood.

Billy had a fierce loyalty to the Englishman and swore vengeance. At Steel Springs, he and others, calling themselves "Regulators," captured Frank Baker and Bill Morton, two suspects in the killing of Tunstall. The pair tried to escape and were gunned down by the posse. A couple of weeks later in Lincoln, Billy organized an ambush that killed Sheriff Brady and Deputy Sheriff George Hindman. Three days later, at Blazer's Mill, "Buckshot" Roberts, a member of the Murphy-Dolan gang unwittingly wandered into the Regulators' camp. A gunfight ensued and Roberts was mortally wounded after killing one Regulator, Dick Brewer.

The feud reached its climax with a gun battle that began July 15, 1878, at the McSween house in Lincoln. During the first three days Billy, the McSweens, and ten gunmen holed up in the sprawling house surrounded by Jimmy Dolan's gang.

On the fourth day Army troops under the command of Lt. Col. Nathan Dudley, from nearby Fort Stanton, were called in to force a cease-fire. The far-reaching power of the Santa Fe Ring was evident. Army cannons and Gatling guns were trained on the McSween house and both sides were ordered to cease firing. The men in the McSween house, vastly outnumbered, obliged. But Dudley's soldiers allowed a couple of Dolan's men, Jack Long and a deaf-mute known only as "Dummy," to slip up and set fire to the house. George Coe, one of Billy's comrades, spotted the fire starters as they left and opened up with his Winchester. Long and "Dummy" ducked inside an outdoor privy and slid down the hole. Coe kept them pinned them down for an entire afternoon.

Legend says that while the battle raged, Susan McSween calmly played *Home Sweet Home* on the piano while Billy the Kid provided the vocals. As the fire progressed, they moved the piano from room to room and kept the music going.

When darkness came, Billy and his friends broke

from the burning house. Several were killed or wounded, but Billy came through without a scratch and escaped. Alexander McSween was among the dead.

Five Tunstall-McSween-Chisum men died in the fight; the Dolan gang lost only one. This turned out to be the last battle of the Lincoln County War, and Billy returned to his outlaw ways.

In 1880, Pat Garrett, a lanky ex-buffalo hunter, was elected sheriff of Lincoln County. In the past, Garrett and the Kid had been friends, drinking, womanizing, and gambling in the cantinas of New Mexico.

By December, Garrett was hot on Billy's trail. On the 19th, Billy and his friends rode into Fort Sumner to celebrate and were greeted by gunfire. Billy's best friend, Tom O'Folliard, was killed. The others escaped.

Four days after the fight, Garrett caught up with the gang at an abandoned cabin at Stinking Springs. Garrett had ordered Billy shot on sight. When the posse saw Charlie Bowdre wearing a hat similar to Billy's, it opened fire. Bowdre fell, mortally wounded. Billy, Dave Rudabaugh, Billy Wilson, and Tom Pickett surrendered later that day.

Billy was tried and sentenced to hang on May 13, 1881. He spent several months in a jail cell above the Lincoln courthouse. One of his guards, Bob Olinger, taunted and abused Billy.

On the evening of April 28, while Sheriff Garrett was away collecting taxes, Olinger took the other prisoners across the street to eat. Billy remained at the jail with a deputy, Jim Bell. Billy asked to go to the outhouse behind the jail. On the way back to the jail, Billy managed to slip off one of his handcuffs. When he reached the top of a

PAT GARRETT

stairway, Billy swung around, hitting Bell in the head with the empty cuff. In the ensuing struggle, Billy got Bell's pistol. Bell turned to run and Billy shot him dead.

Earlier in the day Deputy Olinger had jammed a shotgun in Billy's face. Now Billy picked up that shotgun and went on the balcony to wait for Olinger. As Olinger rushed back to the jail, Billy opened up with both barrels. The deputy fell to the ground mortally wounded. Billy helped himself to a Winchester and a six-gun. He broke the chains of his shackles with a pickax, exchanged pleasantries with some locals, then rode out of town.

He might have made a run for the border and found refuge in Mexico, but he chose to return to his old haunts at Fort Sumner and perhaps to see one of his girl friends — Celsa Gutierrez, Paulita Maxwell, Nasaria Yerby, or Manuela Bowdre. It seems the likable Kid had lovers in every town.

The citizens of Fort Sumner were tight-lipped when the subject of Billy the Kid came up, but Garrett got a tip that Billy was hiding there.

On the night of July 14, 1881, Garrett and two deputies, John Poe and "Tip" McKinney, slipped into town and waited at the Maxwell house. Around midnight Billy got hungry and headed for Maxwell's porch, where a slab of beef was hanging.

Billy stumbled into the two deputies and backed into Pete Maxwell's bedroom, where Garrett was waiting. Billy saw the outline of a man in the darkened room. He pulled his pistol and asked, *"Quien es? Quien es?"* (Who is it?) Those were his last words. Garrett shot him in the heart.

Several of the Kid's friends accused Garrett of murder. Among the most vocal critics was paramour Celsa Gutierrez. Ironically, Celsa's sister, Apolinaria, was married to Pat Garrett.

Garrett was not lionized for killing Billy the Kid. Some said he took unfair advantage by shooting Billy in the dark. He lost the next election for sheriff.

Garrett felt compelled to tell his side of the story. He decided to have a friend, Ash Upson, ghostwrite a biography of Billy. Unfortunately, Upson created myths about Billy's early life. The book flopped, dashing Garrett's hopes of getting rich, but it did build on the legend of Billy the Kid.

Still, Billy remained a relatively obscure outlaw until Walter Noble Burns recreated him into a swashbuckling hero in 1926, with the publication of *The Saga of Billy the Kid*. The book was a bestseller, and a host of imitations followed.

Pat Garrett's own death would have chagrined him. He was shot in the back while relieving himself. His assassin, Wayne Brazel, claimed self-defense.

There was some talk that Billy wasn't killed that night, that he and Garrett were in collusion. In 1948, a man calling himself "Brushy Bill" Roberts surfaced, claiming to be Billy the Kid. He told a convincing story and even went before the governor of New Mexico and requested a pardon. For an uneducated man, Brushy Bill knew more about the Lincoln County War than most historical experts.

Through the years, several old timers claimed to be the real Jesse James or Billy the Kid. In Jesse's case, a scientific examination of his remains in 1995 proved that the man shot in the back by Robert Ford was, indeed, Jesse James.

Many believe Butch Cassidy and the Sundance Kid didn't die in a furious gunfight with Bolivian soldiers but lived out their lives under assumed names.

Famous gunfighters tended to avoid confrontations with other famous gunfighters. A gunfight between legends such as John Wesley Hardin, Jesse James, Billy the Kid, and Hickok would have been interesting, but they seem to have always given each other a wide berth.

A story is told that when Jesse James stopped over in Wild Bill Hickok's town, he sent a message that he would make no trouble, but if the marshal made an attempt to arrest him, a coffin in his size had already been ordered. Hickok never came calling.

John Wesley Hardin claimed he subdued Hickok in Abilene in 1871, using the "Road Agent Spin," when the marshal asked for his guns. But we have only Hardin's word on that, and he said it after Hickok was dead.

Doc Holliday and Johnny Ringo nearly shot it out in Tombstone before they were separated.

A staple in Hollywood's version of the Old West has the young wannabe gunfighter trying to make a reputation by challenging the famous old gunfighter to a duel. In reality, few could muster the courage to pick a fight with some well-known man-killer. It would be like walking up to Jack Dempsey in his heyday and offering to exchange punches.

The real gunfighters were content to let others embellish their exploits. Many, like Hickok, assisted the embellishment, and this usually was enough to scare off challengers.

A story is told that while Hickok was serving as Ellis County sheriff in 1869, he walked the streets of the tough, boisterous town of Hays City armed with a Bowie knife, pistol, and shotgun. That didn't deter a little Irishman named Sullivan who decided to make a reputation. He jumped from an alley with a six-gun aimed at Wild Bill's head. "I've got you now, Hickok," he shouted confidently, "and I'm going to kill you."

Sullivan turned his attention to the gathering crowd, failing to notice Hickok's hand slide down to his pistol. In a flash, Hickok sent a fatal bullet into the would-be gunfighter. "He talked his life away," Hickok commented dryly.

The old time gunfighter may not have been as quick on the draw as modern-day fast draw artists. Electronic timing devices and Fastair missile cameras have recorded speeds of .05 of a second. Old timers tested their speed by placing a coin on the back of the hand at chest level, then tilting the hand until the coin fell. At that moment the hand went for the gun, drew and fired before the coin hit the ground. This takes about .40 of a second. Also, the modern-day artists start the draw with their hands only a few inches away from the pistol butt, or about twice as close as the old timers.

One of the fastest shooting stars to come out of Hollywood was Kelo Henderson. In 1959, he co-starred in a television Western series called *Twenty-Six Men*. The show was filmed in north Phoenix, around 40th Street and Camelback. Phoenix had a population of some 430,000 in those days. The series heralded the daring deeds of the famed Arizona Rangers. Henderson could clear leather, cock, and fire in .27 of a second.

Gunfighters needed more than the ability to shoot fast and straight. Almost anyone who practiced enough could learn to draw and hit an inanimate object or animal. But a special kind of coolness was required for someone to shoot quickly and straight at another human who was shooting back. Add the ability to make split-second decisions and you have the essence of a real gunfighter.

Bat Masterson wrote that of the three most important things for a gunfighter, speed was third and accuracy second. The most important thing, he said, was mental — the ability to make quick decisions and stay cool under fire. Hesitation might cost a man his life, Masterson said, adding that a strong killer instinct was required.

Wyatt Earp said the most important thing was to "take your time — in a hurry!"

Arizona Ranger Lieutenant Harry Wheeler had the abilities cited by Masterson and Earp. Wheeler was one of the best with a gun in a tight situation, but he let his guard down on the streets of Benson one day in 1907 while attempting to arrest a troublemaker named J. A. Tracy.

Tracy got off the first shots. The first bullet went through Wheeler's coat; the second hit the lawman in the leg. Wheeler fired four rounds, hitting Tracy four times. Lowering his gun arm, Tracy said, "I'm all in. My gun is empty."

The wounded Ranger dropped his gun to the ground and advanced to aid his mortally wounded foe. Tracy raised his gun and fired twice. One shot hit Wheeler in the foot. Wheeler grabbed a handful of rocks and hurled them at Tracy, throwing off his aim and giving the Ranger time to wrestle him to the ground.

As both men were lying wounded on the ground, Wheeler looked at a bystander, grinned, and said: "Well, it was a great fight while it lasted, wasn't it, old man?"

Billy the Kid also possessed coolness, and he demonstrated it on several occasions.

One night in Fort Sumner, Billy had a run in with a braggart and bully named Joe Grant. Grant had been drinking heavily and was looking for a fight. Billy walked up to him, noted the ivory-handled pistol in his holster and asked if he could have a look at it. Grant obliged. Billy noticed there were only three cartridges in the cylinder. He spun it around, so the empty chambers would be next on the rotation, and handed it back.

Later the two exchanged hot words. Billy turned to walk out the door and heard the click of a hammer coming down on an empty shell case. Billy spun around, drawing his six-gun, and fired three shots into Grant's head. Billy then walked out the door saying, "Joe, I've been there too often for you." It was said a half-dollar could cover all three of Billy's shots.

Wyatt Earp thought Hickok was unsurpassed as a marksman. Bat Masterson considered Earp the best when it came down to shooting at a man who was shooting back. Earp's testimony at Judge Wells Spicer's hearing after the O.K. Corral fight said a lot about coolness under fire:

"When I saw Billy Clanton and Frank McLaury draw their pistols, I drew my pistol. Billy Clanton leveled his pistol at me, but I did not aim at him. I knew that Frank McLaury had the reputation of being a good shot and a dangerous man, and I aimed at Frank McLaury. The first two shots were fired by Billy Clanton and myself, he shooting at me, and I shooting at Frank McLaury. ... My first shot struck Frank McLaury in the belly. He staggered off on the sidewalk but fired one shot at me."

Several years ago Gene Wilder made a movie about a Jewish gunfighter called *The Frisco Kid*. It was a spoof, but it caused one to wonder if there were any Jewish gunfighters in the Old West. There was at least one, Jim Levy, who was born in Dublin, Ireland. He came to America, where he took a job as a miner in Pioche, Nevada.

A career change was forced upon Levy after he witnessed a murder. When the accused, Mike Casey, told the coroner's jury he shot in self-defense, Levy publicly disputed the claim. An angry Casey then challenged him to a gunfight. Levy wasn't armed so he rushed off to get a six-gun. He returned and fired a bullet that creased Casey's skull. Casey charged so Levy shot him again, inflicting a mortal wound in the neck. Dave Neagle, one of Casey's friends, fired his pistol, hitting Levy in the jaw. On his deathbed, Tom Gasson, the man Casey shot, bequeathed $5,000 to the man who would avenge his death. Levy collected it.

Levy's fame as a gunfighter grew as he traveled to towns such as Virginia City, Leadville, Deadwood, Cheyenne, and Tombstone. He usually worked as a hired regulator and professional gambler. Levy would survive 16 gunfights.

One day in Cheyenne he got into an argument over a game of chance with a local gunfighter named Charlie Harrison. Soon both were spoiling for a fight. When the two met in the street for the classic shoot-out, Harrison drew his weapon in a rush and launched a spectacular display of fireworks. Levy took his time and fired one bullet through the haze of gun smoke, dropping Harrison.

Levy eventually settled in Tucson, where on June 5, 1882, he got into an argument with John Murphy over a game at the Fashion Saloon. The two hurled insults, but since Levy was unarmed, the dispute ended without gun play. Afraid to face the notorious Levy in a gunfight, Murphy and two pals, Dave Gibson and Bill Moyer, decided to set an ambush. Later that night, as the unarmed Levy was leaving the Palace Hotel, the trio sprang from the shadows and gunned him down. Gibson and Murphy eventually were acquitted. Moyer was sentenced to life at the Yuma Territorial Prison.

Despite the violent image of the West there were fewer fatalities in the history of some raucous cow towns than in a typical Hollywood shoot-'em-up. Between 1870 and 1875 only 45 men died by violence in the major Kansas towns of Abilene, Ellsworth, Dodge City, Wichita, and Caldwell.

Now that the trail dust has settled and the false-front saloons are gone, the mystique and the reality of the gun-fighter remains enshrined in the popular culture of the Old West. The last paragraph of Jack Shaffer's classic, *Shane*, best describes the mythical knight in dusty leather that we have come to know as the gunfighter:

"He was the man who rode into our little valley out of the heart of the great and glowing West and when his work was done, rode back again whence he had come and he was Shane."

CHAPTER TWO

Guns Of The Gunfighters: The Tools of Justice and Destruction

————————

A S THEY USUALLY WERE IN A BATTLE, THE TEXAS Rangers dismounted and assembled in a defensive position. Outnumbered four or five to one, the Texans fired their single-shot rifles at a Comanche band.

Then the Texans did a strange thing. They mounted for a charge.

"Powder-burn them!" shouted Ranger Captain John Coffee Hays as the 15 Texans charged through the Comanche ranks, whooping and firing their revolvers. The Comanches had never experienced such a tactic. The charge routed them into retreat and the Rangers chased them for miles in Neuces River country.

Later, the Comanche chief lamented, "I will never again fight Captain Hays, who has a shot for every finger on his hand." A Lipan Apache ally, Chief Flacco, said of Hays, "Captain Jack ... not afraid to go to hell by himself."

That battle in 1844, a year before Texas was annexed into the United States, perhaps was the first charge by a military unit against Indians.

A little earlier that year, Hays and his Rangers armed with revolvers stood off 80 Comanches at the Pedernales River, killing 42. Only two Rangers were wounded.

Until those battles, Indians with bows and arrows maintained superior firepower over their white adversaries. A warrior could unleash 12 to 15 arrows in the time it took to reload a single-shot muzzleloader. Indians planned their tactics accordingly. They would attack to draw fire from single shot weapons and then attack again before their enemy could reload.

But Sam Colt's new revolving pistol changed that, giving the Texans the opportunity to fight as a cavalry unit.

One of the wounded at Pedernales was Samuel H. Walker, who later wrote Colt, praising the revolver. Walker mentioned that the Rangers' "confidence in them is so unbounded, so much so that they are willing to engage four times their number."

Oddly, the pilot's wheel of a sailing ship inspired the idea for what was to become the Western six-shooter. Continuing the oddity, the Republic of Texas Navy was among the first to buy revolvers from the man who invented and developed them — Samuel Colt.

That string of events began in 1830 and culminated in 1873 with the introduction of the Peacemaker.

The Peacemaker — officially called Colt's Single Action Army Revolver — became the favorite pistol model of gunfighters. Costing $17 through a mail-order catalog, the handgun was well-balanced, durable, and had "more curves than a dance hall girl." The Peacemaker was available in two barrel lengths, 7 1/2 inches and 4 3/4 inches. Gunfighters generally preferred the shorter barrel.

Fully loaded, it weighed just three pounds but packed a wallop. It fired .45 caliber (255 grain) bullets propelled by 38 to 40 grains of black powder.

Some three decades earlier, the U.S. Army rejected Colt's revolvers. But the Army kept the Peacemaker as its official sidearm until the 1890s. Before choosing it, the Army rigorously tested several revolvers. Other brands were superior to the Colt in some tests, but for overall ruggedness, reliability, and simplicity of design, none could compare with the Colt.

Although it was designed for close-quarter fighting, the pistol could be effective at long range. The Army found that to allow for trajectory the point of aim at 150 yards should be four feet above the target, and at 200 yards one had to line the sights up eight feet above the target.

Colt got the idea for a revolving cylinder in 1830 when he was working aboard a sailing ship bound for Calcutta. The inspiration came from a clutch that aligned spokes on the pilot's wheel with mechanism linking it to the rudder. Applying this principle, he eventually developed a revolving pistol with a cylinder that would bring chambers in line with the hammer and barrel. He patented the invention in England in 1835 and in the United States the following year — the year that the Alamo fell.

The first Colts, produced between 1836 and 1841, were "belt" or "holster" revolvers in calibers ranging from .28 to .36 and were manufactured at a plant in Paterson, New Jersey. They came in barrel lengths ranging from 4 to 12 inches but the 7 1/2 and 9-inch models were the most popular. They were fragile and fired only five rounds.

The U.S. Army rejected the revolvers, believing common soldiers were not intelligent enough to shoot anything more complicated than a single-shot muzzleloader. Colt did sell some revolvers to the Texas Navy in 1839. Some of them found their way into the hands of the legendary Texas

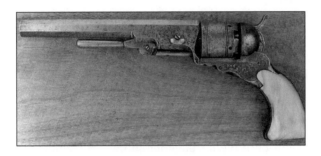

TEXAS PATERSON COLT, 1836

Rangers, who were waging war against the formidable Comanche and Kiowa warriors.

Despite the popularity of the pistol among Texans, the Colt company failed in 1842, two years before the Rangers showed the revolver's value in mounted warfare. Neither the U.S. military nor the general population would buy Colt's revolvers. But, in 1846 the Mexican War created a new demand for Colt revolvers.

General Zachary Taylor commanded American forces at battles such as Palo Alto and Resaca de la Palma and forged deep into Mexico. Two of the soldiers in his command were from the ranks of the Texas Rangers — John Coffee Hays, now a colonel, and Sam Walker, a captain.

Walker had realized that the revolver needed more durability for use on the frontier and had been in touch with Colt, suggesting improvements. General Taylor dispatched him to expedite the production of 1,000 revolvers on a $28,000 contract.

When the order was placed, Colt had to advertise for some of his own creations as he had sold or given away all his samples. He gathered a few old Patersons and began work on a weapon to meet Walker's specifications. The result was the famous model 1847 Walker Colt, a .44 caliber pistol weighing 4 pounds 10 ounces.

Unlike the Paterson, it had a trigger guard and had only five moving parts. Carrying six rounds in the cylinder, the Walker was the West's first six-shooter. More like a hand cannon than a pistol, it fired a 219-grain bullet and 50 grains of black powder. It was the most powerful pistol ever built until the introduction of the .44 Magnum. One of the drawbacks of the Walker Colt was that it was so powerful that on occasion it would blow itself apart.

The order revived Colt's gun business. Although he had no production plant, he enlisted the aid of Eli Whitney to manufacture the revolver. They produced 1,100 pistols. Soon Colt was able to open his own plant and introduce a new model, the 1848 Dragoon. This pistol was slightly modified from the Walker and fired a 40-grain bullet.

In 1850, a new, lighter model, the Navy .36 caliber pistol, weighing just 2 pounds 10 ounces and firing six shots, became a favorite of the Forty-Niners.

Prior to the Civil War, Colt wanted to design a pistol that combined the light weight of the Navy with the power of the Dragoon. The result was the Colt model 1860 Army. Over two hundred thousand of these were produced. It was the standard sidearm of both Union and Confederate soldiers and was used in the Army until the introduction of the legendary Peacemaker in 1873.

One of the reasons for the Colt's popularity out West was that if any part of the weapon was broken, it would still function. Texas Ranger Captain John (Rip) Ford wrote that during the Battle of the Frio in 1866, the hammer of Ranger Sam Walker Trimble's (this writer's great-grandfather) Colt revolver broke and he was still able to fire his weapon by using a small hand-held tack hammer to strike the percussion cap.

In the hands of a skilled gunfighter, the Colt six-shooter was both a tool of justice and destruction. Sometimes it was referred to as "Judge Colt and his jury of six."

Gunfighters usually carried only five loaded cartridges in the cylinder, letting the hammer rest on the empty one. This writer can attest to the foolishness of letting the hammer rest on a live round. I became a believer one day when my pistol slipped from my hand, the hammer struck a sidewalk and a bullet chipped the plaster off a wall a couple of inches from my ear.

Those who relied on the six-gun for livelihood would hone the action on their six-gun to a whisper.

Some gunfighters tried to increase their firepower by fanning the weapon — filing back or holding down the trigger and brushing the hammer continuously with the left hand to achieve rapid-fire. Wyatt Earp claimed he had never seen a gunfighter fanning his pistol, nor did he know of any of the great ones who shot from the hip. He also dismissed the carving of notches on the handle for each victim as a creation of the pulp writers.

The art of pulling the pistol from the holster in a hurry was to bring the hand straight back, from a forward position, laying the thumb on the hammer and cocking it while sliding the weapon out and into a shooting position. If the shooter tried to pull his pistol by coming from a perpendicular position, the result could be a badly damaged thumb. That's why they called them "thumb-busters."

The two-gun fighter was mostly a creation of Hollywood. Few could do anymore than waste ammunition with their off-hand. Even the ambidextrous Hickok wasn't as good with his left hand. During a shooting exhibition when the left hand didn't perform as well as the right, his only comment was he'd never shot a man with his left hand anyway. The real purpose of a second gun was to have a weapon in reserve. In the early days of the revolver, extra weapons were carried because it took a painfully long time to reload. If they didn't carry extra pistols, they had an extra cylinder or two loaded and ready to insert.

Holsters came into use in the Army during the 1840s. Their primary use was to protect the weapon and provide a secure place during travel. Flaps covered the butt to keep sand and dust out.

The earliest holsters were slung from the saddle. When the boys came home from the Army, some cut the flap tops off their holsters and used a leather thong to loop over the hammer to keep the pistol secure.

Holsters were worn high on the hips in a variety of ways designed both for comfort and a quick draw. The most popular holster was the Mexican loop where the top and back were not cut off but folded over and down behind the holster to form a belt loop and a skirt between the holster and the wearer. The backing has one or two slits cut into it where the holster slides through to keep it secure

Holsters were worn on the left or right side. The cross-draw was common in the 1850s and '60s. A right-handed man would wear his pistol on the left side, butt forward. It was easier to draw while sitting or riding horseback. In the Army a right-handed man wore his pistol on the right side, butt forward and many carried that habit over into civilian life. Some preferred to wear a shoulder holster, while others used a belt swivel. Some cowboys had holsters sewn in their chaps.

A few wore two holsters, butt forward or backward.

Many gunfighters disdained the use of holsters, preferring instead to line their pockets with fine buckskin for quick, easy release.

Wild Bill Hickok wore his ivory handled .36 caliber silver-plated Navy Colts butt-forward in a red sash tied around his waist, while John Wesley Hardin preferred a shoulder holster. Hardin also designed a vest lined with leather pockets for smooth withdrawal and wore his pistols butt-forward for a cross-draw.

Many gamblers preferred to carry a Derringer tucked away in a vest pocket or a boot holster. Others just tucked it in their waist band. Prostitutes also carried the Derringer for protection against unruly customers. They found the crotch pouch to be a convenient place to carry the little shooter. Holsters were usually worn waist high. The low-slung buscadero fast-draw holster so popular with the shooting stars of Hollywood was uncomfortable when walking, riding or sitting.

Despite the fact that getting the pistol into a shooting position in a hurry was important, emphasis on the fast draw was more a product of the 20th century. In the Old West, when a fight was imminent, a gunfighter usually had his weapon drawn and ready to fire. Gunfighter Clay Allison put it best: "Speed is fine, accuracy is final."

A gunman was considered proficient with a revolver if he could hit what he was aiming at in a distance of fifteen yards. At fifty yards it was considered good shooting to group the shots in a six-inch circle.

Hickok's reputation may have been exaggerated, but

he was an excellent shot. He put a bullet in the heart of Dave Tutt from 75 yards away.

Wild Bill frequently put on public exhibitions to show off his marksmanship. He could walk and alternately fire with each hand, keeping a tin can dancing in front of him. Old timers claimed Wild Bill could group his shots within five inches from a distance of fifty yards. A friend of Hickok's said he could toss a can 15 feet into the air, draw his pistol, and put two holes in the can before it hit the ground. Still another claimed he saw the shootist put six pistol balls into a letter O on a signboard some sixty yards away — without sighting the pistol with his eye. Wyatt Earp said he saw Hickok do the same thing in Kansas City from a hundred yards.

Stories that shooters like Wild Bill could keep a tin can dancing to the rhythm of gunshots are not beyond possibility, but one should remember that after a few shots the smoke would have been so thick it would have been difficult, if not impossible, to even see the tin can.

The history of firearms in the West began with flintlocks and muzzle-loading Kentucky long rifles along with the popular rifles made by the Hawken brothers of Missouri. They were the weapons of choice from the time of Lewis and Clark to the Mexican War.

A flint and striker was used for hundreds of years to ignite the powder charge behind the lead ball in the old muzzle-loading weapons. A piece of flint was attached to the hammer. A small load of powder was placed in a pan next to the breech. When the trigger was pulled, the flint would come forward, hitting a striker and throwing sparks into the pan. The powder in the pan would explode in a flash and send fire into a hole in the breech, exploding the powder inside the barrel and thrusting the bullet to its intended target.

The technique didn't always work. Sometimes the result was nothing more than a "flash in the pan," adding a phrase to the American lexicon.

Next came the percussion cap. In 1807, a Scottish clergyman named Alexander Forsyth mixed a concoction of fulminate of mercury and niter, which would explode when hit by a hammer. Then, in 1814, an American artist, Joshua Shaw, harnessed the energy in a little copper cap that was placed on a nipple located at the breech of the weapon. When hit with a hammer, the cap would explode sending a charge through a hole in the nipple to the larger powder charge in the breech. The resulting explosion (usually) sent the lead ball or mini-ball through the barrel towards the target.

Today, modern day mountain men relive those days staging shooting contests with their flintlock and percussion cap weapons and they still wage friendly arguments over which ignition system is best.

Among the first breech-loading rifles was one invented by Major Patrick Ferguson, an officer in Washington's Revolutionary Army. It could be loaded and fired six times in a minute. Ferguson demonstrated the rifle that bore his name in June, 1776. Four years later he was killed at the Battle of King's Mountain in North Carolina.

Rifles began to change dramatically by the mid-19th century. In 1848, Christian Sharps invented the breech-loading Sharps caliber rifles that were favorite of the plains men of the West and of both Union and Confederate soldiers during the war. Sharpshooters could pick off a

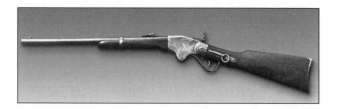

SPENCER CARBINE

sniper at 800 yards. "It could be fired today and kill tomorrow," claimed one old timer.

With that rifle, the word, "sharpshooter" became part of the American lexicon.

In 1874, buffalo hunter Billy Dixon became a legend when he blew a Comanche warrior off his horse with a Sharps .50 caliber at the unbelievable distance of 1,538 yards, or about 7/8 of a mile.

Plains men could load and fire five rounds in a minute in the breech-loading Sharps, a far cry from the old muzzle-loaders that took the best part of a minute to load and fire one round.

Despite the popularity of the Sharps rifles, there was a great need for a repeating rifle. During the Civil War, teenager Christopher Spencer invented the first lever-action repeating rifle. At first the Army wasn't interested, saying it was too complex for the average soldier. But Spencer was able to get President Lincoln to test fire the rifle and he ordered the Army to purchase more than 100,000.

The rifle loaded seven shells in the stock and one in the barrel. Rebs said enviously that the Yanks had a rifle that could "load on Sunday and fire all week." General U.S. Grant called the Spencer the "best rifle in the hands of the troops at the end of the war."

It's interesting to note that after the Civil War ended the Army called in the repeating rifles and issued breech-loading single-shot Springfields to the troops. Custer's Seventh Cavalry was carrying these at the Battle of the Little Big Horn in 1876. The Indians had them outgunned that day with some 700 Winchester repeaters.

For any long-range shooting, the legendary Winchester 73 was the favorite. It was truly the fighting rifle of the old civilian West.

The Winchester 73's ancestor was the Henry rifle, patented in 1860 by a genius named B. Tyler Henry. The rim-fire rifle fired fifteen shots plus one in the barrel. The rifle was loaded at the muzzle end through a tubular magazine under the barrel. It had a problem with dirt and grit getting into the open slot of the magazine.

Again, the conservative military minds thought it "too complicated" for ordinary soldiers and purchased only 2,000 Henrys. Private organizations also purchased and used them in the war. Those units lucky enough to be issued the Henry enjoyed a tremendous firepower advantage over their Confederate foes.

In 1866, Winchester produced the famous "Yellow Boy," so-called on account of its brass receiver. The most popular was the 24-inch octagonal barrel (the carbine had a round 20-inch barrel). Improvements over the Henry model included a side load gate at the magazine for insertion of cartridges. It fired a .44-28 rim-fire cartridge but didn't pack a lot of punch.

In the 1873 model, the Winchester was stronger, simpler and lighter. The mechanism was improved and the brass receiver was replaced with an iron one. The .44-40 center-fire rifle fired fifteen shots plus one in the chamber.

The 40 grains of powder gave the bullet a lot more punch. It was the first truly practical center-fire repeating rifle. It came with a 12-shot, 20-inch barrel or a 15-shot, 24-inch barrel. The rifle was such a success the company continued to produce them until 1919.

The Winchester rifle was so popular the name became synonymous with any rifle in the West. A story is told that during a strike at a Remington arms factory, loyal employees came to work with "their trusty Winchesters" — a phrase so natural that no one questioned it.

In 1878, the .44 caliber Colt came on the market. It was popular among Westerners who also carried the Winchester Model 1873, a .44-40 caliber rifle. That way, one needed to pack only one kind of ammunition for both pistol and rifle.

Reading the pulp Westerns, one would conclude that the Colt revolver was the only pistol used in the Old West. Remington built fine six-shooters. In 1858 Remington produced a single-action revolver with a solid-frame strap over the cylinder which gave more strength and a continuous sighting groove. Five years later a new model came out with several modifications that resulted in the popular .44 caliber New Model Army.

At times Wyatt Earp carried a Smith & Wesson. Frank James packed an 1875 model Remington and also owned a Smith & Wesson Schofield, as did his brother Jesse. Buffalo Bill Cody was also a great admirer of the Smith & Wesson revolver. Besides his Colt, Jesse James carried a .44 Starr revolver.

Starr came out with a revolver during the war that was more rigid than the Colt and had a top strap across the cylinder similar to the Remington. It was also easier to break down to remove the cylinder. Despite this, the .44 Starr never did gain universal appeal among Westerners.

Black powder was used until the 1890s and it threw out large puffs of white smoke that could quickly engulf a saloon. That might explain why some of the shooting seemed so poor.

A gunfight in the Long Branch Saloon in Dodge City on April 5, 1879, is a good example. Cockeye Frank Loving and a buffalo hunter named Levi Richardson got into a row, chasing each other around a gaming table, shooting all the while, their pistol barrels almost touching. Richardson, fanning his pistol, fired five rounds and missed five times. He did succeed in setting Cockeye Frank's clothing on fire. His clothes trailing smoke, Cockeye finally hit Levi with a fatal bullet.

Before the advent of metallic cartridges in the 1850s, the re-loading of cap and ball pistols was slow and could have fatal results. Consequently, Westerners carried extra cylinders loaded and ready to fire.

There were many ways a man could get his whiskers singed — or worse. Stray powder around the cylinders could set off a chain fire where all the cylinders fired at once. To prevent this, grease was packed in the chambers with the charge. Many a frontiersman earned the nickname "Broken-hand" or "Black-face" after his weapon blew up on him.

The earliest cartridges were made of paper. In fact, the word cartridge comes from the Latin word, *carta,* or paper. For some 300 years before the Civil War, soldiers were wrapping their powder in paper packets. All they had to do was to roll the paper with a "former," or round stick to make a cylinder similar to a roll-your-own cigarette. They tied or "choked" one end with a string, removed the round stick, dropped in a lead ball, and tied it off with string.

Next to go into the paper cylinder were sixty grains of black powder. The cylinder was bent back towards the bullet and tied it off. Although a soldier could make them, the arsenals supplied cartridges in cases of 10.

Mountain men and frontiersman prided themselves on being able to "guesstimate" the amount of powder needed, thus eliminating the need for paper.

The first metallic cartridges were rim-fire and did not pack much of a wallop. They consisted of lead and powder packed in a copper cartridge. Around the rim on the head of the cartridge was fulminate of mercury, which would explode when hit by a hammer.

But one couldn't always count on the cartridges to explode. When Jack McCall shot Wild Bill Hickok in Deadwood on August 2, 1876, every cartridge misfired except the first one — the one that fired the fatal bullet.

Inventors kept experimenting on new kinds of cartridges. The result was the center-fire cartridge that is still in use today. With development of center-fire, cartridges became more powerful. The legendary Winchester 73 was the first truly practical center-fire repeating rifle.

An interesting story is told about how the Native Americans contributed to the evolution of cartridges. After the Civil War as the rails were building west, the Army was sent out to protect the construction crews. Some Sioux warriors managed to capture a few of the new breech-loading .50 caliber rifles that were intended for the soldiers. The Army placed an embargo on selling bullets to the Indians. Undaunted, the Sioux gathered up empty shell

COLT '73 PEACEMAKER

casings — the old solid-head type — and punched holes in the heads. They crammed a percussion cap into the hole. A tiny rock was dropped in the casing to act as an anvil to explode the cap. Next, they filled the case with powder and stuck a lead ball on the end. The result was a reloaded cartridge. For a time the indignant Army brass was trying to figure out how the Sioux were shooting their captured rifles when bullets were impossible to obtain. The clever Sioux creation turned out to be the progenitor of the modern-day center-fire cartridge.

In 1872, Colt patented an entirely new revolver. The cartridges were loaded and extracted from a side gate in the recoil shield and the ejector was housed alongside the barrel. It retained many of the characteristics of the old Colt but had an entirely new design. The result was the New Army Model of 1873 — the Peacemaker — the most popular revolver of them all.

The most deadly defensive weapon for close range undoubtedly was a shotgun. Lawmen kept them stashed conveniently in saloons for emergencies. Few troublemakers were foolish enough to stand up against a lawman packing a sawed-off 10-gauge. Lookouts in gaming casinos packed them. So did stagecoach guards, giving us the term "riding shotgun" for sitting in the seat opposite the driver. They were also popular with Wells Fargo messengers riding the express cars during the heyday of the train robbers.

According to one account, legendary lawman Jeff Milton's life was saved and a train robbery was thwarted by a shotgun at Fairbank, Arizona, on February 15, 1900. "Three-Fingered" Jack Dunlap, Bravo Juan Yoas, and other members of Burt Alvord's gang attempted a daring daytime robbery at the Fairbank station.

Milton was standing in the open door of the express car when the gunmen opened fire, severing an artery in Milton's arm. He fell backward behind a trunk, bleeding profusely. As the outlaws charged toward the car, Milton rose up and cut loose with a twin-barrel 10-gauge shotgun. Dunlap took a fatal dose of buckshot. His partner, Bravo Juan, had just enough time to turn around and retreat. He took a load in the seat of his pants.

Wyatt Earp:
The Showdown
in Tombstone

*The 'legend' of Wyatt Earp began after he died
with the publication in 1931 of a book. Scores of
books and articles followed, and yet historians and
others continue trying to determine exactly what
happened — and why — during a 30-second street
fight that has captured the interest of the world.*

———

O N   A   COLD,   GRAY   OCTOBER   AFTERNOON   IN   1881,   FOUR
armed men strode purposefully down Tombstone's
Fremont Street. Snowed had fallen briefly the day
before, and a brisk chill lingered in the air. All four were
well-dressed. Three of the men, brothers, bore a striking
family resemblance — light brown hair, tall, strapping,
drooping mustaches — and wore long, dark frock coats
over business suits. The fourth man was slightly built,
shorter than the others, with a sweeping mustache and ash
blond hair. In contrast to robustness of the other three, his
face appeared emaciated. He was wearing a long, gray
overcoat he had purchased the day before. Concealed
inside the coat was a sawed-off shotgun.

Down the street, between Camillus Fly's photograph
gallery and the Harwood house, six men dressed in cowboy
garb waited and talked quietly.

WYATT EARP

A feud that had been brewing between these two groups for several months. Mostly the feud had involved exchanges of threats. But the time for talk had ended. The grim-faced men didn't know it at the time but they were heading for a rendezvous with destiny. The events that followed would be frozen in time and etched in blood in the chronicles of Western history.

No one knows for certain who made the first move. Street fights are like that. But, all hell broke loose. For about 30 frenzied seconds there was blurred movement as shots rang out and acrid, white smoke filled the air.

When the smoke cleared, three men lay dead on the ground. Three others were wounded. Only one man walked away unscathed. His name was Wyatt Earp.

Historians and Old West buffs still study and discuss what has become known as the Gunfight at the O.K. Corral. Most historians agree that the Earps came closer to representing law and order than the group who opposed them, an amoral band of rogues known as the "Cowboys."

But, the Earps have their detractors. Some claim they were really "bad guys" who schemed and stole under the guise of a peace officer's badge and bullied the unarmed Cowboys into a showdown.

The question persists: Did either side really want to fight at that particular place and time?

Sure, the Clantons and McLaurys had been boasting that they were going to shoot the Earps on sight but it sounded more like bravado over hurt pride. Also, they were still waiting for some members of the gang to arrive. And, as they later demonstrated, they would rather ambush their foes than take them on in a stand-up fight.

Town Marshal Virgil Earp, the man in charge of the other side, was carrying a cane, hardly a weapon to use in a gunfight. And as the shooting commenced, he shouted, "Hold, I don't want that!"

But fate was dealing the hands, and likely some movement on one side or the other set the event in motion. We're still searching for "truth." Perhaps that's why the Gunfight at the O.K. Corral still holds our interest.

Wyatt Berry Stapp Earp was born in Monmouth, Illinois, on March 19, 1848, the third of five sons born to Nicholas and Virginia Ann Earp. He was named for Wyatt Berry Stapp, his father's commanding officer during the Mexican War.

The oldest son, James, would suffer serious wounds

during the Civil War. Although he traveled to the West with his brothers, he didn't participate in the gunplay.

Virgil, the stalwart, was the leader, but Wyatt was the most influential in the brotherhood. Their father had instilled a strong sense of family loyalty in the boys. They were clannish and didn't make friends easily. None was a hard-drinker. The Earp brothers also inherited a strong sense of adventure and restlessness from their father.

Wyatt also had a younger sister, Adelia, born in 1861, and an older half-brother, Newton, born in 1837.

The four youngest boys, Virgil, Wyatt, Morgan, and Warren would live by the code of the gun. Warren and Morgan would die by the gun. Virgil would be crippled permanently by gunshot wounds in an ambush. Although he faced death on several occasions, Wyatt was never so much as scratched by a bullet.

Wyatt Earp was not considered a legend during his lifetime. Others, such as Wild Bill Hickock, Bill Cody, Billy the Kid, John Wesley Hardin, and Jesse James, were better known. The street fight near the O.K. Corral was almost forgotten in the annals of the Old West. Wyatt died peacefully in 1929, after the West had passed into the realm of myth and legend. It was after his death that books, movies, and television resurrected — and sometimes reconstructed — his deeds, elevating him to superstar status.

Wyatt Earp belonged to the West, unlike many of his contemporaries, the Eastern dandies who "wested" seeking fame, adventure, and fortune then rushed back East to tell their stories to some eager journalist or pulp writer.

As a youngster, Wyatt crossed the wilderness to California with his family. As a teenager he drove freight wagons over a treacherous 400-mile road from the port at

San Pedro to Prescott, Arizona. During the late 1860s, Wyatt was working as a teamster on railroad construction. On occasion he labored as a boxer, a trade that would prove useful in his later line of work.

The lawless towns young Wyatt frequented were inhabited by track layers and hunters. Many of them were violent products of the Civil War who knew how to shoot and fight and had no compunction against killing. Saloons served a fiery, tangleleg whiskey that could peel the hide off a Gila monster, or make a man go crazy.

Wyatt drifted across much of the West during his early twenties.

In 1870, at the age of 22, he married Urilla Southerland in Lamar, Missouri. He was elected town constable, barely beating his half-brother Newt. It was the only elected office he ever held.

His wife died shortly after they were married, and Wyatt spent the next couple of years drifting. In Kansas City he made the acquaintance of Wild Bill Hickock and some of the well-known buffalo hunters of the time including the legendary Billy Dixon. Listening to their tales inspired Wyatt to head west and hunt buffalo. He was hunting buffalo in the early 1870s when he met Bat Masterson. The two would strike up a fast friendship and would later work as lawmen in Dodge City. They remained friends until Masterson died in 1921.

Wyatt was invited, but declined, to go on the hunt with Billy Dixon and Bat Masterson in 1874, thus missing the famous fight at Adobe Walls against Quanah Parker's Comanche warriors. This was the battle where Dixon made his famous long shot. Using a .50 caliber Sharps, Billy Dixon shot a Comanche saddle from the unbelievable distance of 1,538 yards. Not surprising, it was the last shot of the fight — the warriors withdrew.

Like many of his kind, Wyatt wasn't always on the right side of the law. In April, 1871, a warrant was sworn for his arrest for stealing horses in the Indian Territory. He was not convicted of the charges and the matter seems to have been dropped.

Next Wyatt headed for Kansas, where his interests turned to gambling. During the next few years he worked as a peace officer and gambler in Wichita and Dodge City. Professional gamblers worked a circuit that included the Kansas cow towns at trails' end and the military posts around payday. Cowboys and soldiers eager to try their luck were easy marks for the gamblers. It was in 1877, on one of these gambling sojourns to Fort Griffin, Texas, that Wyatt met Doc Holliday.

John Henry Holliday was born in 1852 in Griffin, Georgia, into a prosperous Southern family. He became a dentist but had to quit his practice when his body was wracked by tuberculosis. He headed west in hopes the dry climate might prolong his life. Along the way he paired up with Kate Elder, better known as "Big Nose" Kate. Their relationship was volatile. She could down a glass of whiskey as fast as he could. Their drunken battles were epic.

Kate was resourceful. Wyatt told a story about his first meeting with Holliday at Fort Griffin when Doc was playing cards with a man named Bailey. Doc caught Bailey cheating and told him to "play poker." In gambling lingo, this was a polite way to say, "Quit cheating." Bailey didn't take heed and Doc pulled in the pot. Bailey went for his gun, but Doc pulled a knife and planted it in Bailey's brisket. The town marshal and his constables confined Doc in the lobby of a local hotel while a band of angry citizens outside were planning a necktie party. When Kate learned of Doc's predicament she tied a couple of horses behind the hotel and set fire to a nearby shed. Then she hollered "Fire!" When everybody's attention was diverted, Kate pulled a gun on the lawmen and rescued her lover.

Wyatt and Doc maintained a long friendship. Wyatt said that the bond was established when Doc backed his play one night in Dodge City. A couple of Texas cowhands named Driskill and Morrison were on the prod, threatening Wyatt. They cornered him just outside the Long Branch Saloon. Doc was playing cards inside when he heard the ruckus. He grabbed his six-shooter and pushed through the swinging doors. The Cowboys were distracted long enough for Wyatt to slap his pistol barrel on Morrison's head. When one of the Cowboys' friends took a shot at Wyatt, Doc plugged him in the shoulder.

"One thing I've always believed," Wyatt said later. "If it hadn't been for Doc Holliday, I'd have cashed in that night."

The Earps, especially Wyatt and Morgan, were among the few people Doc could call friends. The irascible, cantankerous Holliday highly valued this friendship.

Bat Masterson said, "His whole heart and soul were wrapped up in Wyatt Earp and he was always ready to stake his life in defense of any cause in which Wyatt was interested."

Wyatt's tolerance of Doc during his bouts with booze and violent outbursts was a credit to his patience. Also, Doc's association with some shady characters would embarrass Wyatt in the months to come. Many of Wyatt's problems in Tombstone were the result of his being friends with or defending Doc.

In 1880 the raucous silver camp on Goose Flat that folks were beginning to call Tombstone was experiencing prosperity unsurpassed in the history of Arizona. The great silver strike prompted talk of creating a state with Tombstone as the capital. Some 2,000 would-be millionaires pitched tents, wickiups, and shanties, and they set about the business of getting rich without working. Saloons and gambling halls on Allen Street were open for business 24 hours a day.

Tombstone became a gathering place for a frontier society ranging from mining and real estate speculators, entrepreneurs, merchants, preachers, and teachers to prostitutes, cattle rustlers, con men, and tin horn gamblers.

Like many others, the Earp brothers came to Tombstone by way of Prescott. James, Virgil, Wyatt, and Morgan arrived in December, 1879, and began investing in mining claims, town lots, and water rights. They were accompanied by their wives, or traveling companions, Bessie, Allie, Mattie, and Louisa respectively. Doc Holliday and Big Nose Kate remained in Prescott and didn't arrive in Tombstone until the following September.

Virgil Earp had been a peace officer in Prescott for a couple of years prior to moving to Tombstone and was persuaded by U.S. Marshal Crawley P. Dake to take a deputy marshal's position in Tombstone. During his first few months in Tombstone, Wyatt worked a job riding shotgun for Wells Fargo. On July 27, 1880, Pima County Sheriff Charlie Shibell appointed Wyatt deputy for the Tombstone district. (Cochise County, where Tombstone now is located, was formed in the following February.)

Since there were no courts in Tombstone, there was little a lawman could do, so it's likely the sheriff wanted a deputy to collect taxes. In those days, the sheriff received 10 percent of the taxes collected in his county, and the rich silver mines provided a good source of revenue.

The rugged terrain in southeastern Arizona near the Mexican border was an ideal place to hide stolen cattle. Ranchers on both sides of the border were victimized by a loosely organized pack of thieves under the leadership of a hard-bitten rascal known as "Old Man" Clanton.

Newman Haynes Clanton and his sons — Ike, Billy, and Phineas (known as Phin) — along with brothers Tom and Frank McLaury, used their ranches as clearinghouses for stolen cattle in the San Pedro and Sulphur Springs Valleys. Others in the gang, which numbered about 50, included Frank Stilwell, Johnny Ringo, and William Brocius Graham, whose alias was "Curley Bill Brocius."

Stilwell had held up so many stagecoaches, it was said, that the stage company's horses were more familiar with his voice command to "halt" than they were with the company drivers'.

Ringo, according to legend, was a deadly, moody, morose gunfighter who quoted Shakespeare. In reality, he was a two-bit saddle bum who never killed anyone. Like many others of his ilk, Ringo's reputation was self-inflated to instill fear in any potential enemy.

"Curly Bill" was a tall, bushy-haired rogue with coarse features. But he exhibited a gregarious nature that made him popular in Cochise County. Beneath that sunny disposition was a cold-blooded killer. Newspapers at the time hailed him as the "most famous outlaw in Arizona."

After Old Man Clanton was killed in an ambush in

July, 1881, Curly Bill assumed leadership of the Cowboys.

One of the great ironies of Cochise County history was that many of the area's most notorious outlaws came to Arizona in the late 1870s from Texas as cowhands working for John Slaughter, later one of Arizona's great lawmen and a deadly enemy to cattle rustlers. Among them were Stilwell, Ringo, Curly Bill, and Billy Claiborne (sometimes spelled Claibourne or Clairborne).

Stealing livestock wasn't the gang's only activity. They preyed on Mexican smugglers along the border and stagecoaches rumbling along the lonely roads loaded with bullion from the mines or payroll for the miners.

The outlawry was so brazen that cattle were being rustled in daylight. The rush of population to Tombstone created a beef bonanza and meat contractors and butchers didn't care whose brand was on the cows they bought.

Wyatt saw himself more as a lawman than tax collector. He let the word out to the outlaws that law and order would be maintained. The Cowboys took up the challenge and stole Wyatt's horse.

In mid-July, 1880, some mules were stolen from the Army at Fort Rucker, in the Chiricahua Mountains. Lieutenant J. H. Hurst rode into Tombstone and asked Wyatt for assistance in recovering the animals. Wyatt, Virgil, and Morgan — along with the officer and four soldiers — tracked the mules to a ranch on Babocomari Creek owned by Tom and Frank McLaury. Word was passed from the ranch to Lieutenant Hurst that the mules would be returned only if the Earp brothers left.

There were 15 or 20 rustlers holed up at the ranch, so Wyatt said he and his brothers would leave. But he warned the officer that the Army still wouldn't get its mules. Wyatt's assessment was correct. The Cowboys did not keep their word, and Hurst went home empty-handed.

Before Hurst left, the McLaury brothers told him to warn Wyatt that if he and his brothers "interfere with us again, we'll shoot you on sight."

"Tell 'em they'll have their chance," Wyatt replied.

A few weeks later Wyatt met the McLaury brothers on the streets of Charleston. "That army officer give you our message?" Frank asked.

"He did," Wyatt replied, "but in case you didn't get my answer, I'll repeat it."

The McLaurys turned and walked away, making threatening remarks.

A few days after the confrontation at the McLaury ranch, Lieutenant Hurst accused the McLaurys in a local newspaper of stealing government property. Frank McLaury responded by accusing the officer of stealing the mules. Accusing the accuser was a practice the outlaws would use to tarnish the Earps' reputation in the months to come. Some of the well-orchestrated charges inspired by Texas attorney Will McLaury, an older brother, continue to taint the Earps' reputation to this day.

It was about this time that Wyatt, acting on a tip, found his horse in Charleston in the possession of young Billy Clanton. Earp stared the kid down — it was said he had eyes that could burn holes right through a man. Clanton surrendered the horse and his guns, all the while threatening to "get" Wyatt at some later date.

Trouble erupted again on an October evening in 1880 when Curly Bill and some of his friends were firing their pistols in Tombstone, a violation of the town ordinance.

When city Marshal Fred White attempted to arrest Curly Bill, the outlaw offered his pistol to the lawman butt forward. Then he spun it around and shot the officer in a maneuver that became known as the "Curly Bill spin."

At the sound of gunfire, Wyatt borrowed a pistol and rushed to White's assistance. Arriving just as the lawman was shot, Wyatt "buffaloed" or knocked Curly Bill out with a blow to the head with the pistol barrel. As the outlaw chieftain was dragged off to jail, a few of his friends, including the Clantons and McLaurys, shot a few poorly aimed rounds in Wyatt's direction.

Later, a lynch mob gathered, but Wyatt dispersed the crowd. Surprisingly, Marshal White, on his death bed, exonerated Curly Bill, saying he believed he was shot accidentally. Others would claim Marshal White's killing was intentional because he had countered some local politicians involved in a real estate scam, and they wanted him out of the way.

Once again, Wyatt Earp had stirred the ire of the Cowboys.

By late 1880, Earp was embattled on two fronts. On one side, vengeful Cowboys regarded him as a threat to their free rein. On the other, Earp had gotten crossways with the local political machine. Wyatt, a Republican, didn't support Sheriff Charlie Shibell's bid for re-election and resigned as Pima County deputy sheriff on November 9, 1880. Shibell appointed Johnny Behan as Wyatt's replacement in the Tombstone district.

Behan was a gregarious political hack who was more interested in padding his pockets than enforcing the law. He also was on friendly terms with the Cowboys because they let him win at poker. They liked him because he took a *laissez-faire* approach to their cattle rustling.

Political scandals in the boom town brought rise to a Citizens Safety Committee, a group made up mostly of businessmen dedicated to restoring law and order, one way or another. Throughout the West, vigilance groups such as Tombstone's were organized when citizens felt the law was not doing enough to thwart crime.

By early 1881, Republicans led by Mayor John Clum controlled Tombstone's City Hall. With Democrats controlling the county and Republicans running the city, there were many political clashes. Clum also was editor of the Republican organ, the *Tombstone Epitaph.*

Not to be denied, the Democrats had their own paper, the *Tombstone Nugget,* owned by local politicos John Dunbar and Harry Woods. Woods and Johnny Behan, along with Dunbar's brother Tom, had been members of the territorial Legislature and had acted to create Cochise County in the rich Tombstone district.

In the months before the O.K. Corral fight, these two papers reported events with partisan prejudice. Clum's *Epitaph* trumpeted law and order, the Citizens Safety Committee, and its enforcers, the Earp brothers. The *Nugget* supported Behan and the county ring. And, as the donnybrook between the Cowboys and Earps mounted, the *Nugget* embraced the Cowboys as playful youngsters out having fun.

In February, 1881, soon after Cochise County was created, the Democratic Party machine persuaded territorial Governor John C. Frémont to appoint Johnny Behan as sheriff, the highest-ranking political office in the new county. Wyatt Earp had coveted the appointment. Being a Republican, Earp seemed likely to get the job from the

Republican governor. But, Behan had political connections with Tom Dunbar, a territorial delegate, and his brother John. The Dunbars enlisted a powerful friend, Congressman James G. Blaine, to ask the governor to appoint Behan. Blaine was to become secretary of state when the administration of President James Garfield was sworn in on March 4, 1881. No doubt, he had little trouble persuading Frémont to appoint Behan.

Behan's cronies, Harry Woods and John Dunbar, became undersheriff and treasurer respectively. All would have to stand election in the fall.

Wyatt planned to run for sheriff of Cochise County against Behan in the fall but withdrew when Behan promised to make him undersheriff and let him share the tax-collecting perks. Behan later reneged on his promise, saying "something" made him change his mind. That "something" had to do with a dark-eyed beauty named Josephine Sarah Marcus.

Josie Marcus, the daughter of a prosperous Jewish merchant in San Francisco, wanted to be an actress. Against her parents' wishes, the headstrong woman joined an acting troupe doing Gilbert and Sullivan in the boom towns.

Johnny Behan first met her in Prescott. Quite smitten, he followed her to San Francisco and used all his charm to lure her into moving to Tombstone with him. Under promise of matrimony she finally agreed and even hocked her jewels to buy a house for them. Unwisely, she put the house in his name, something she would later regret.

Behan resumed his womanizing habits, and Josie broke off the relationship. One day she chanced to meet Wyatt. He was everything a young woman dreamed of, except he was "married" to Mattie Blaylock, the woman who had traveled with him from Dodge City.

Wyatt didn't let his "arrangement" with Mattie keep him from courting Josie. And Josie responded to him.

Johnny Behan never forgave Wyatt for taking up with Josie. He became determined to even the score with Wyatt, even if it meant openly siding with the Cowboys.

Josie is one of the unique characters in this frontier drama. She had the distinction of being paramour to the feud's chief antagonists. And she did tell her story, published under the title *I Married Wyatt Earp.*

Josie provides some good insight into the close relationship between the sheriff and the outlaw element in Cochise County. While she was living with Behan, the Cowboys, including, Johnny Ringo and Curly Bill Brocius, frequently came to the house to play poker.

The event leading directly to one of the West's most famous gunfights occurred on March 15, 1881, when the Benson stage, carrying several thousand dollars in silver bullion, was fired upon by four masked men at Drew's Station, about a mile north of Contention City on the San Pedro River. Scheduled to ride shotgun that fateful night was Bob Paul. The driver was Eli "Budd" Philpot.

Fate took a strange twist when Philpot got sick and handed the reins over to Paul. Philpot was mistaken for the shotgun guard and was shot and killed by one of the bandits. The stage sped away as the bandits fired on it. Another shot entered the back of the stage, fatally wounding passenger Peter Roerig.

When word of the robbery reached Tombstone, a posse that included Wyatt, Virgil, and Morgan Earp, Bat

Masterson, and Sheriff Johnny Behan was formed. They tracked one of the outlaws, Luther King, to a ranch where he was captured without incident. The frightened prisoner identified his accomplices as Bill Leonard, Jim Crane, and Harry Head. All were known members of the Cowboys.

They stole some cattle and drove them along to cover their trail. The posse kept up relentless pursuit for more than two weeks, covering hundreds of miles and enduring great hardship before giving up the chase.

Luther King didn't stay behind bars long. He had been turned over to Sheriff Behan, who turned him over to Undersheriff Harry Woods, who turned him loose. Woods, the editor of the *Tombstone Nugget*, claimed that King escaped while he and John Dunbar, Behan's partner in a livery stable, were making out a bill of sale for King's horse. Actually, King walked out the back door of the jail, where a horse was waiting. He went to Mexico.

Throwing up a smoke screen, Undersheriff Woods, in a newspaper article on the holdup, blamed it on Doc Holliday. The politicos figured that by blaming Holliday they could discredit his pal Wyatt Earp in the race for sheriff.

Holliday responded typically, saying that if he had pulled the job he would have gotten the loot.

Town gossip was the only thing linking Doc to the robbery until one night when he got into a fight with Big Nose Kate. Sheriff Behan saw an opportunity and got her drunk enough to sign an affidavit stating Doc was one of the stage robbers.

A warrant was issued and Doc was arrested. Wyatt posted the $5,000 bail. Big Nose Kate sobered up the next day and confessed she didn't know what she had signed. The charges were dropped. Doc gave Kate $500 and told her to get out of town. She went to another mining town, Globe, where she used the money to make the down payment on a small hotel.

But the damage was done. The accusation against Doc Holliday was an embarrassment to Wyatt Earp's law and order political campaign. Wyatt decided the best way to vindicate his friend and get his political campaign back on track was to capture the stage robbers himself. And that set into motion a chain of events that led directly to the Gunfight at the O.K. Corral.

Wyatt decided to enlist the services of Ike Clanton to capture the stage robbers. Clanton was known to have a leaky mouth and a penchant for getting others in trouble. Clanton was the Judas that Wyatt needed.

Meeting in secret on the afternoon of June 2, 1881, at the Eagle Brewery Saloon, Wyatt offered Clanton the $6,000 reward Wells Fargo had posted for the capture of the stage robbers. All he had to do was lure Leonard, Crane, and Head to a pre-arranged site where Wyatt could make the arrest. Four days later Clanton met with Wyatt and wanted to cut Frank McLaury and Joe Hill in on the deal. He also wanted to know if Wells Fargo would pay the reward whether the robbers were captured or killed. Wyatt checked with Wells Fargo agent Marshall Williams, who telegraphed the company office in San Francisco. Word came back that the reward would be paid if the outlaws were dead or alive.

There was another reason for Clanton's willingness to go along with the plot. Bill Leonard had a ranch that Clanton coveted. After the robbery, Clanton, thinking Leonard had left the country, moved onto the ranch. When

Leonard made it clear he was staying around, Clanton figured setting him up for the Earps would not only get him the ranch free but also the reward money.

On July 4, Clanton, Joe Hill, and Frank McLaury reported to Wyatt the whereabouts of Head and Crane. The plotters would lure the wanted men to the Bisbee road, where Wyatt could arrest them. The trap had to be delayed, however, due to a prior commitment.

That prior commitment occurred a few days later when a gang of Cowboys, including Old Man Clanton, his sons Ike and Billy, Joe Hill, Johnny Ringo, and Tom and Frank McLaury, massacred a party of Mexican smugglers in Skeleton Canyon. Eight Mexicans were killed and $4,000 in coins and bullion was taken. Although the Cowboys bragged openly about their escapade, no charges were brought against them. They went on a drinking and spending spree that lasted until the loot was gone. It probably took another few days for them to get over the hangover.

In August, friends of the slain Mexicans took their revenge. Near the border they spotted Old Man Clanton and several other men, including Jim Crane, driving a herd of cattle to Tombstone. The Mexicans laid an ambush of their own, killing all but one. Among the dead were Old Man Clanton and Jim Crane.

When Joe Hill reported to Wyatt the death of Crane, Earp sent the outlaw in search of Harry Head and Bill Leonard. Hill arrived at their New Mexico hideout and learned both Leonard and Head had been killed in a foiled holdup attempt at a store owned by the Haslett brothers. Soon after, Curly Bill and some of the boys murdered the Hasletts in revenge.

MORGAN EARP

Morgan Earp was dispatched to New Mexico to verify the story. He learned that Leonard had made a dying confession, saying that he, Crane, Head, and King had robbed the stage, and Crane had fired the shot that killed Philpot.

The three Judas Cowboys, Ike Clanton, Frank McLaury and Joe Hill, had lost their blood money. Wyatt also came up empty-handed, losing his chance to capture the stage robbers.

Nothing might have come of the secret deal between Wyatt and Clanton except that Wells Fargo agent Marshall Williams had seen Wyatt showing the telegram from the home office in San Francisco offering a reward, dead or alive. Williams really didn't know anything about the deal as he walked up to Ike Clanton in a saloon one night and chided him for betraying his outlaw cronies. Clanton, who had been drinking heavily, blabbed the whole story.

Later, Clanton confronted Wyatt and accused him of

confiding their deal with the Wells Fargo agent. Wyatt denied the accusation. Clanton then claimed Earp must have told Doc Holliday. Wyatt again denied telling anybody.

The confrontation was loud and several people heard the talk of Clanton's betrayal. Clanton liked to say "Fight was his racket." Josie Earp wrote years later, "He should have said 'racket was his fight.'"

Doc Holliday was in a cantankerous mood when he learned of Ike's accusations. Doc valued loyalty, and Bill Leonard was an old friend. He angrily rebuked Clanton, then challenged him to get a gun and make a fight of it. The two were separated by Wyatt and Virgil. For political reasons, the last thing the Earps wanted was a gunfight.

Later that evening, a drunken Ike Clanton threatened Wyatt. Wyatt dismissed the threats and told Clanton to go home and "sleep it off." But, as the saying goes, "the fat was in the fire."

Ike's situation was getting desperate. His double-cross was out in the open and he was good as dead if he didn't convince the outlaw hierarchy, now led by Curly Bill Brocius, that Wyatt had deliberately lied to stir up trouble among the Cowboys. He twisted the tale enough to buy some time. The only way Clanton could get back in the good graces of the gang would be to force a showdown with the Earps.

During the next several days Clanton made several threats against the Earps, growing more brazen with each shot of whiskey. During these displays of bravado, Clanton always made sure he was unarmed.

Another stage robbery, this one on the road between Tombstone and Bisbee, occurred on September 8. The stage driver identified the bandits as Pete Spence and one of Johnny Behan's deputies, Frank Stilwell. It was believed that Curly Bill and Pony Deal were nearby.

During the holdup, one of the robbers asked the passengers if they had any "sugar." Stilwell always referred to money as "sugar." Also he had left some distinctive boot tracks at the scene.

A few days later, Stilwell and Spence were arrested by a posse that included Wyatt and Virgil Earp, Marshall Williams, Fred Dodge (an undercover Wells Fargo agent), and another Behan deputy, Billy Breakenridge. Stilwell and Spence men posted bail and were released.

Naturally, the Cowboys were outraged at being bested again. A few nights later in Tombstone several Cowboys including Tom and Frank McLaury, Ike and Billy Clanton, Johnny Ringo, and Joe Hill, accosted Morgan Earp, who was alone and unarmed.

"I'm telling you Earps something," Frank McLaury said. "You may have arrested Pete Spence and Frank Stilwell, but don't get it in your heads you can arrest me. If you ever lay hands on a McLaury, I'll kill you."

"If the Earps ever have occasion to come after you," Morgan replied, "they'll get you." Then he turned and walked away.

On October 22, Ike and Billy Clanton and Tom and Frank McLaury went to Charleston to obtain the release of Billy Claiborne. A few months earlier, on July 14, 1881, Pat Garrett had gunned down the notorious Billy the Kid, and now Claiborne was proclaiming himself the new "Kid." A cocky, Cowboy wannabe, he was in jail for killing an unarmed, drunken man who had been heckling him in a saloon.

Meanwhile, in Tombstone, Ringo, Curly Bill, and friends

were saying that the Earps' days were numbered. Interestingly, by the afternoon of October 25 most of them, including Ringo and Curly Bill, had left town. That evening Ike Clanton and Tom McLaury joined an all-night poker game in the Occidental Saloon. The players were an unlikely bunch, considering the events of the past few months. They included Virgil Earp, Johnny Behan, Ike Clanton, and Tom McLaury. It's likely none realized what the day would bring.

On the morning of that fateful day, Wednesday, October 26, 1881, Wyatt was awakened by Ned Boyle, who passed on Ike Clanton's latest threats: "As soon as those Damned Earps make their appearance on the street today, the ball will open. We are here to make a fight. We are looking for the sons of bitches."

Later that morning, Clanton again threatened to kill the Earps and Holliday on sight. Virgil Earp, sleeping off the all-night poker game, was awakened and told Clanton was on the street, armed with a pistol and a Winchester, telling passersby, "As soon as the Earps show, the ball will open."

Clanton then entered Fly's boarding house, where Doc Holliday was sleeping. Mrs. Fly warned Big Nose Kate that Ike Clanton was armed and looking for Doc. When awakened, Doc replied, "If God will let me live long enough, he will see me."

Virgil Earp, well-aware of Clanton's threats, walked up to him and grabbed the rifle barrel. When Ike swung around, Earp slapped him alongside the ear with his pistol barrel.

Virgil asked if he was looking for him and Clanton

replied, "Yes, and if I'd seen you a second sooner I would have killed you."

Clanton was hauled into court and fined $27.50 for violating gun ordinances. Virgil then deposited Clanton's pistol and rifle at the Grand Hotel.

A few minutes later Wyatt met Tom McLaury on the street and challenged him to make a play. When Tom refused, Wyatt slapped him with his pistol barrel. Then, Wyatt boldly followed Ike Clanton and the McLaury brothers into Spangenberg's gun shop. While they were rearming, Earp noticed Frank McLaury's horse was on the boardwalk, another violation of city ordinances. Wyatt grabbed the animal by the bit and backed him into the street. Frank charged out and a heated argument ensued. The Cowboys backed away, then headed for Dunbar's livery stable.

Meanwhile, the Earps gathered in Hafford's Saloon and were awaiting developments when representatives of the Citizens Safety Committee offered to help fight the Cowboys. Virgil declined the offer. Then, Johnny Behan walked in and had a drink with Virgil. Behan refused Virgil's offer to join him in making an arrest of the Cowboys. Instead, Behan offered to go down and disarm them. Behan headed back for another visit with the Clantons and McLaurys.

At about 2:45, the Earps left Hafford's Saloon. Virgil had decided to make the arrest after being informed the Cowboys were on the street and armed.

As the Earps walked north on Fourth Street, they were joined by Doc Holliday. He was carrying a cane, which he traded to Virgil for a sawed-off shotgun. Virgil and Wyatt walked in front, followed by Morgan and Doc. At

Fremont, they turned left, heading west towards Third Street, and spread out in a line.

Sheriff Behan stepped up and said, "Hold up, boys, don't go down there or there will be trouble; I have been down there to disarm them."

The group ignored him and walked grimly on. Believing the sheriff had not disarmed the Cowboys, Virgil slid his pistol from the front of his waistband around to the left side. He switched the cane from his left hand to his right. Wyatt put his pistol in his overcoat pocket.

When the Earps and Holliday were a few feet from the Clantons and McLaurys, Virgil spoke: "Throw up your hands, boys, I intend to disarm you."

Billy Clanton and Frank McLaury both had their hands on the butts of their pistols. Tom McLaury was standing next to his horse with his hand on a Winchester in a scabbard. Virgil heard the sound of hammers being cocked and said, "Hold on, I don't want that!" The time was 2:47 p.m.

Wyatt saw Billy Clanton go for his gun, but, knowing Frank McLaury to be the more dangerous, drew his pistol and shot Frank in the stomach. McLaury fell backward, clutching his abdomen.

Billy hurried his shot and missed Wyatt. "The fight," as Wyatt later testified, "then became general."

When the shooting began, Tom McLaury's horse started dancing around, preventing him from pulling the rifle from the scabbard. He then jerked a pistol from inside his shirt and fired two shots. He lost his cover when his horse spun away, and Doc Holliday cut him down with a double load of buckshot. Tom, gasping for breath, staggered over to the corner of Fremont and Third where he fell, fatally wounded. Doc dropped the shotgun and jerked his pistol and swung it towards Frank McLaury.

Virgil switched the cane to his left hand, pulled his revolver, and fired one round at Frank McLaury and three at Billy Clanton. Ike Clanton, claiming he was unarmed, ran up and grabbed Wyatt by the left arm.

Wyatt glared at him. "This fight has commenced," he said, "go to fighting or get away." Ike Clanton turned and ran, finally hiding behind a barrel of mescal in a dance hall several blocks away.

Meanwhile, Billy Clanton shot Morgan. The bullet entered Morgan's shoulder on one side and passed through, barely missing the spine. Morgan went down, but he fired and hit Billy in the abdomen. Billy fired again and hit Virgil in the calf. Virgil staggered but fired three times, hitting Billy twice, in the wrist and the left breast.

Seriously wounded, Frank McLaury staggered into the street, then paused, laid his pistol barrel across his left forearm and aimed at Doc Holliday.

"I've got you now," he said.

"Blaze away! You're a daisy if you do!" Holliday replied, firing his pistol, hitting Frank McLaury in the left breast. McLaury fired at the same time, creasing Holliday.

Morgan, on the ground seriously wounded, drew a bead on Frank and dropped him with a shot to the head.

Billy Clanton, game to the end, lay mortally wounded, asking for more bullets. Photographer Camillus S. Fly walked over and picked up his revolver. Billy would live for another hour in agony. Just before dying he said, "Good-bye, boys; go away and let me die."

The shooting was all over in less than thirty seconds. More than 30 gunshots were fired.

The Vizinia Mine whistle blew, signaling a gathering of the Citizens Safety Committee. Just after the gunfight, Ike Clanton was arrested and taken to the county jail. The *Tombstone Nugget* would report concern over the safety of Clanton. Apparently there was talk of lynching him.

Why Clanton had chosen to run instead of fight that day is open to conjecture. It was his big mouth that ignited the fireworks. He talked the talk but when it came time to walk the walk or "ride the river," he backed down and ran for his life. No doubt he was unarmed. His guns were at the Grand Hotel. Perhaps he was expecting help from Ringo, Curly Bill and a few other gunmen that day and when he had enough friends to support his play, he would have gone to the hotel and gotten his guns. And when they didn't show, he lost his nerve. Maybe he was expecting a fight at 3 o'clock and the Earps got there early.

Billy Claiborne, the self-proclaimed "Billy the Kid," had run away when it looked like the fight was going to be more than just talk. Months later his tough talk would prove fatal. The hot-tempered Claiborne would challenge Buckskin Frank Leslie and be gunned down in Tombstone.

After the O.K. Corral fight, Sheriff Behan attempted to arrest Wyatt, who glared at him and replied, "I won't be arrested now. You threw us, Johnny."

The dead men were dressed in suits and placed in caskets in the window of Ritter and Evans funeral parlor. Next to the bodies, friends placed a sign that read: "Murdered on the Streets of Tombstone."

Three days after the gunfight, Mayor John Clum temporarily suspended Virgil Earp as city marshal, pending investigation of the gunfight. That same day Ike Clanton

VIRGIL EARP

filed murder charges against the Earps and Doc Holliday.

Judge Wells Spicer began hearings on the gunfight on November 2. Johnny Behan testified first. He was either lying through his teeth or was incredibly oblivious to what had been going on for the past several months. His testimony also contained a number of convenient "I don't remembers."

Two days later Will McLaury, an older, half-brother of Tom and Frank, and a prominent lawyer from Fort Worth, Texas, arrived and joined the prosecution team. McLaury was able to get Wyatt and Doc locked up without bail. Morgan and Virgil were exempted because of their wounds. Wyatt and Doc spent eighteen days behind bars. Fearing assassination by friends of the slain men, heavily armed members of the vigilance committee maintained a round-the-clock guard around the makeshift jail where Wyatt and Doc were held.

Will McLaury, seeking vengeance for the deaths of his brothers, would stop at nothing to get the Earps and Holliday. He scripted Ike Clanton's testimony in an attempt to twist the events of the past months and paint the Earps as outlaws who killed the McLaury brothers and Billy Clanton because they feared the "honest cowboys" would expose their nefarious schemes.

The tactic worked well for Will McLaury. The clever lies he and Ike Clanton concocted are still believed by many today, including a few historians. Clanton portrayed the Cowboys at the gunfight as unarmed victims of the brutal Earps. He also accused the Earps of stealing from Wells Fargo then planning the robberies to cover up their thefts.

Clanton's well-crafted tale spun a web of intrigue. According to Clanton, the Earps were in cahoots with the Benson stage robbers — Crane, Head, Leonard, and King. Because the four knew too much, the Earps wanted them dead. Clanton claimed Wyatt told him he had "piped off" the stolen money to Doc Holliday and Bill Leonard.

It's unlikely that Wyatt would have made such a damaging statement to a known outlaw. More important, the stage robbery failed, so all the money was accounted for.

Clanton also claimed the Earps wanted him and Frank McLaury out of the way because they knew too much. Clanton seems to have forgotten that Wyatt had an excellent chance to shoot him point blank at the gunfight. On many of the questions, Clanton too had a convenient case of "I don't remember."

Ike Clanton not only wanted vengeance for the killing of his brother and the McLaurys, but he also desperately needed a plausible story to allow him back into the good graces of the gang. His self-righteous testimony was laden with errors but has been the source used by several writers who sought to debunk the reputation of the Earp brothers.

There were only four stage robberies during the period in question, and in each there is overwhelming evidence that the Earps could not have been involved. Also, Wells Fargo had undercover operatives working in Tombstone. These agents cooperated with the Earps in hunting down the outlaws. They probably would not have done so if there had been the slightest suspicion of unlawful conduct.

There's pretty good evidence to show that Sheriff Behan conspired with the equally vindictive Will McLaury to paint the Earps in a bad light by claiming the dead men were peaceable citizens.

Judge Spicer concluded the hearings on November 29 and ruled the Earps were justified in their actions. Newspapers from New York to San Francisco had been running daily accounts of the hearing. Much of the nation was now focused on the outlawry in Cochise County.

Clanton's uncorroborated testimony, fallacious as it was, did irreparable damage to the Earps' reputation. Most of the debunking of the Earps stems from his twisted tale.

The Cowboys, under the tutelage of lawyer Will McLaury, lost that round. In their minds the court of law had failed them. Now they would use the law of the gun to settle matters.

On December 6, President Chester A. Arthur, in a speech to Congress, deplored the lawlessness of Tombstone and proposed legislation that would allow the U.S. Army to act as a *posse comitatus.*

On December 14, the Sandy Bob stage bound for Benson with Mayor John Clum on board was stopped about three miles out of Tombstone. The stage carried no money and remarks by the bandits indicated they wanted to assassinate the mayor. Clum saved his life by slipping away in the darkness. Threats of assassination included not only the Earps and Holliday, but also Judge Spicer, Mayor Clum, and Marshall Williams.

On the evening of December 28, Virgil Earp left the Oriental Saloon and headed for the Cosmopolitan Hotel where the Earps had holed up since the threats began. As he reached Fifth Street, the resounding roar of shotgun blasts was heard. Virgil, wounded badly in the left arm and bleeding profusely, walked back to the Oriental to tell Wyatt he'd been shot. Virgil was permanently crippled in the attack. His fighting days in Tombstone were over. When Virg's wife, Allie, arrived at the scene, he said, "Never mind, I've got one arm to hug you with."

Immediately after the wounding of Virgil, Marshal Dake swore Wyatt in as a deputy marshal. Wyatt, investigating the shooting, found a hat with Ike Clanton's name on it at the site where the assassins had hidden. He also learned from a night watchman that Ike Clanton, Frank Stilwell, and Hank Swilling were seen running away. All were carrying shotguns. Another witness saw Johnny Ringo running down the street right after the shooting.

Warrants were issued for the arrest of Curly Bill, Frank Stilwell, and Ike Clanton for the shooting of Virgil Earp, but nothing ever came of it. Justice worked in strange ways in Tombstone.

A few days later, on January 6, 1882, the Tombstone-Bisbee stagecoach was robbed again. Frank Stilwell and Pete Spence, still out on bail from the previous robbery, were identified as the bandits along with Curly Bill and Pony Deal. Curly Bill took the guard's shotgun and boasted he'd use a Wells Fargo gun to rob the next Wells Fargo strongbox. He didn't waste any time. The next day the Tombstone-Benson stage was held up again. Curly Bill and Deal were identified as the culprits.

Since tampering with the mail is a federal offense, U.S. Deputy Marshal Wyatt Earp went in hot pursuit of the outlaws. The Cowboys, however, were too well organized for Wyatt to have any luck. Fresh horses were readily available at rustler lairs throughout the vast region.

The new town marshal, Dave Neagle, was lax on enforcing the gun ordinances that had been imposed by Virgil Earp. Once again the Cowboys were riding high in Tombstone. They took up headquarters at the Grand Hotel.

A small group of intrepid gunmen with colorful-sounding names like Turkey Creek Jack Johnson, Texas Jack Vermillion and Sherman McMasters, along with a few stalwart members of the Citizens Safety Committee, remained loyal to Wyatt.

Territorial Governor John C. Frémont had been forced to resign, and acting Governor John Gosper proposed large rewards for the capture of the outlaws. Marshal Dake recommended that Wyatt head a special posse to rid the county of the Cowboys gang. Johnny Behan tried to abort the effort by re-opening the case against the Earps. He persuaded a judge in Contention City to oblige. The Citizens Safety Committee, fearing the Earps would be assassinated, demanded they be allowed to provide escort and be present at the trial. A trial judge, however, refused to hear the case.

On the evening of March 18, tragedy struck again. Wyatt and Morgan were in Hatch's pool hall after attending a show at Schieffelin Hall. Morgan was shooting pool and

Wyatt was sitting in a chair nearby. Suddenly, the upper window of the backdoor shattered and two shots rang out. Morgan slumped over the table, mortally wounded by a bullet that shattered his spine. Another bullet just missed Wyatt. Morgan lived just long enough for brothers Jim and Warren to assist Virgil to the scene.

Doc Holliday, crazed for revenge over the murder of Morgan, went on a house-to-house search, kicking in doors, as he unsuccessfully sought Johnny Behan and Will McLaury.

Witnesses testified before a coroner's jury. The most damaging evidence was given by Marietta Spence, wife of Pete Spence. She claimed her husband, along with Frank Stilwell and Florentino Cruz, were the killers. Curly Bill and Ringo were also seen near the pool hall that night. It was rumored that attorney Will McLaury had financed the killing. Also, it was rumored that Johnny Behan knew of the plot.

Wyatt decided the only way justice would be served for the shooting of his brothers would be for him to take the law into his own hands. He would be his brother's avenger, becoming judge, jury and executioner.

Morgan Earp's body was taken to the train at Contention City where family members would escort it to Colton, California, for burial. Wyatt and Doc rode the train as far as Tucson. Wyatt suspected there might be more assassination attempts at the Old Pueblo. When the train pulled into the station at Tucson, he and Doc, along with Warren Earp, Turkey Creek Johnson, Texas Jack Vermillion and Sherman McMasters stood guard.

Suddenly, in the darkness outside the train window, Wyatt caught a glimpse of two rifle barrels shining in the moonlight from behind a flat car. He could make out three or four figures crouched. Wyatt was carrying a shotgun with eighteen slugs in the barrels—enough to get them all. As he was getting into a shooting position the shotgun hit a handrail and made a noise, startling the gunmen. They scattered like quail. Wyatt jumped from the rail car and caught up with one of the men as he rushed across the tracks in the glare of a locomotive headlight. When they were about 30 feet apart Wyatt recognized Frank Stilwell. Wyatt advanced towards Stilwell through the misty steam raised from the locomotive. When they were about 15 feet apart, Stilwell stopped, a frozen look of horror on his face. He looked at the tall man with the sweeping mustache approaching through the mist and said, "Morg!" He hesitated then said again, "Morg!" The next day Frank Stilwell's body was found in the train yard. Cause of death—lead poisoning.

Citizens in Pima and Cochise County followed the turbulent events with interest. George Hand, a Tucson saloonkeeper, recorded in his diary: "Mar. 21. Frank Stillwell (sic) was shot all over, the worst shot-up man that I ever saw. He was found a few hundred yards from the hotel on the railroad tracks. It is supposed to be the work of Doc Holliday and the Earps, but they were not found. Holliday and the Earps knew that Stillwell shot Morg Earp and they were bound to get him."

Before leaving Tucson, the Earp party searched unsuccessfully for Ike Clanton. By this time Ike had become quite adept at hiding.

Unfortunately, the shooting of Frank Stilwell, even though he got what was coming to him, placed Wyatt outside the law. Unless he too could find witnesses to testify that he was miles away at the time of the crime, a practice used with great success by the Cowboys, he was going to stand trial for murder. Wyatt knew if he surrendered to authorities he probably wouldn't live long enough to stand trial. And if per chance he did stand trial, he would likely be the scapegoat for all the violence and incur the wrath of justice.

On March 21, when Wyatt and his followers arrived at the Cosmopolitan Hotel in Tombstone, Johnny Behan was waiting to arrest them.

"I want to see you." Behan said, trying to sound authoritative.

"Johnny, you may see me once too often," Wyatt replied. He had good reason to believe Johnny may have had an indirect role in Morgan's murder. Earlier, Morgan had interceded on a tussle between Johnny and Josie and had knocked Behan to the ground.

A telegram arrived from Tucson authorizing Behan to arrest Wyatt for murder. The telegrapher warned Wyatt, then held the telegram for an hour to give him time to get away. Within the hour, Wyatt and his men rode boldly out of Tombstone.

The next to die was Florentino Cruz, or Indian Charley, as he was known. Cruz had acted as lookout during the assassination of Morgan Earp. He was found at Pete Spence's wood camp in the south pass of the Dragoon Mountains. Before his execution, Cruz admitted getting $25 for the job.

Johnny Behan organized a posse made up of Cowboys that included Ike and Phin Clanton, Curly Bill, and Johnny Ringo. Pima County Sheriff Bob Paul refused to join Behan's posse saying, "He persists in cloaking the most notorious outlaws and murderers in Arizona with the authority of the law. I will have nothing to do with such a gang."

On March 23, Wyatt and his men rode some 30 miles west of Tombstone to Mescal Springs, at the southern end of the Whetstone Mountains. Wyatt planned to camp there while searching the Babocomari Creek area for Curly Bill. He'd gotten a tip that Curly Bill and some of the Cowboys were camped at the springs. They'd been making a long, uphill ride and Wyatt loosened his gunbelt to be more comfortable. They approached the springs in the afternoon and Wyatt dismounted to check for sign. He was holding a shotgun in one hand and his horse's reins in the other. He walked over a rise and stumbled into the outlaw camp. When the shooting started, Wyatt's men, still horseback, spurred their mounts and scattered helter-skelter for cover, leaving him to fend for himself. Curly Bill, who was stirring up a pot of stew, dropped the ladle and grabbed a shotgun. He fired at close range, sending a double load of buckshot that tore a piece off Wyatt's coat. Wyatt raised his scatter-gun and returned the fire, hitting Curly Bill squarely in the midsection with two loads of buckshot.

After the Cowboy chieftain went down, Wyatt turned his attention to the other desperados who were ducking and dodging, firing wildly as they ran for cover. Wyatt dropped the empty shotgun and reached for his pistol, but during the excitement, he'd forgotten the loosened gunbelt, which had slid down around his knees. To make matters worse, his horse, spooked by the gunfire, was doing a war dance. Every time Wyatt would reach down to pull his revolver, the horse would rear, pulling him back up again. The outlaws made their getaway while a pre-occupied

Wyatt and his mount were doing a circle dance. One of the Cowboys' bullets ripped through the horn on his saddle. Wyatt was able get off a few well-aimed shots into a grove of cottonwoods where the Cowboys had sought shelter. Johnny Barnes suffered a gunshot wound from which he would later die.

Four days later, the Earp party rode into Colonel Henry Clay Hooker's famous old Sierra Bonita ranch at the north end of the Sulphur Springs Valley. Wyatt and his men were treated with the generous hospitality for which the ranch was noted. Later that evening they rode on.

The next day Johnny Behan's posse arrived at the Hooker ranch, demanding food and the whereabouts of Wyatt Earp. The rancher told the sheriff he didn't know where Wyatt was and wouldn't tell if he knew.

Behan accused Hooker of "upholding murderers and outlaws."

Hooker responded, "I know the Earps and I know you and I know they have always treated me like a gentleman; Damn such laws and damn you, and damn your posse. They are a set of horse thieves and outlaws."

At this point, Ike Clanton jumped into the fracas saying, "Damn the son of a bitch. He knows where they are. Let's make him tell."

About that time one of Hooker's men drew down on Ike with his Winchester. "You can't come here into a gentleman's yard and call him a 'son of a bitch.' Now you skin it back! Skin it back!"

Behan, never one to fight if there was a way out, backed down.

Hooker was too much of a gentleman to send the posse away on empty stomachs. They were invited to dinner but Behan's outlaw friends were made to eat at separate tables.

Later that evening Behan approached the cowpuncher who'd covered Colonel Hooker and offered him a hundred dollar diamond stud from his shirt if he'd not say anything about the incident. Behan's bribe didn't work. The story later appeared in the *Epitaph.*

Behan tried to secure scouts from nearby Fort Grant but the commanding officer, aware of Hooker's response, refused.

By now, most of the Cowboys involved in the shootings of Virgil and Morgan Earp were either dead or had left the country. Wyatt and his men rode for Silver City, New Mexico, arriving there on April 8. During the next few weeks the *Nugget* printed stories of gunfights, each with an eyewitness account of the killing of Wyatt Earp. Wyatt was next heard from in Gunnison, Colorado. Doc went to Denver.

On May 25, a devastating fire broke out in the Tombstone business district destroying most of the buildings. The Cowboys were prime suspects in the arson.

In June, authorities in Arizona attempted to have Wyatt and Doc extradited from Colorado to stand trial for the murder of Frank Stilwell. Governor F. W. Pitkin, fearing the men wouldn't live long enough to stand trial, refused extradition.

On July 13, the body of Johnny Ringo was found at Turkey Creek, in the foothills of the western slope of the Chiricahua Mountains. Ringo died with his boots off, his undershirt was torn in half and wrapped around his feet. He was found beneath a blackjack oak on the edge of the creek with a bullet in his head. His pistol was hung up on his watch chain with one bullet missing. The watch was still running. A piece of his hair was missing, as if he'd been scalped. A coroner's jury ruled it suicide. Wyatt later claimed he came back to Arizona and killed Ringo. Billy Breakenridge blamed Buckskin Frank Leslie. Others claimed Johnny O'Rourke, better known as "Johnny-Behind-the-Deuce," killed Ringo, and

JOHNNY RINGO

was in turn gunned down by Ringo's pal, Pony Deal, who was in turn iced by somebody else. As for Ringo's murderer, who knows! Johnny Ringo's death remains a mystery.

On November 14, Buckskin Frank Leslie gunned down Billy "the Kid" Claiborne in front of the Oriental Saloon after "the Kid" made some taunting remarks about Leslie killing Johnny Ringo. It would be the last of Tombstone's famous gun duels.

Will McLaury's vendetta had been costly. He later wrote the experience was "very unfortunate — as to my health — and badly injured me as to money matters — and none of the results have been satisfactory — the only result is the death of Morgan and crippling of Virgil Earp and the death of McMasters." Wyatt said Sherman McMasters was not killed until 1898, in the Spanish American War.

Ike Clanton moved his rustling operation north into

the White Mountains. He locked horns with another famous lawman, Commodore Perry Owens. Owens, sheriff of Apache County, set a posse after the Clanton gang in the summer of 1887. Ike was shot and killed while running away (something he was good at) on September 14, 1887, by Rawhide Jake Brighton, a deputy sheriff of Apache County. Phin Clanton was captured and wound up doing ten years in the Yuma Territorial Prison.

That same year, on November 8, Doc Holliday died of tuberculosis in a hotel room in Glenwood Springs, Colorado. Lying in bed that final day, he asked for a shot of whiskey, then looked down at his bare feet and muttered characteristically, "This is funny!"

Johnny Behan, an appointed sheriff and perennial political hack, lost his party's nomination for county sheriff to Larkin Carr. Behan's siding with the outlaw element was too much for the Democratic Party hierarchy and he fell out of favor. Behan was quite adept at padding his expenses and collecting taxes, earning some $25,000 a year as sheriff when the annual salary was only $2,500. He was indicted by a grand jury for continuing to collect taxes after he left office.

Recently, evidence was found in a collection at the University of Arizona that supports the claim that Behan and Ike Clanton were in cahoots. A loan record was found among the collections of the Jacobs family, which owned mercantile stores and provided banking service in southern Arizona. The $500 loan was dated just two weeks after the Gunfight at the O.K. Corral and could have been used to pay legal fees and generate suits against the Earps. According to the ledger, Ike repaid the loan 12 days later.

Behan's political crony, county Treasurer John Dunbar,

was also indicted, but another cohort, Marcus A. Smith, district attorney and future U.S. senator from Arizona, chose not to prosecute. Thanks to the crony system, Behan continued to live off the public trough, eventually becoming a politically appointed superintendent at the Territorial Prison at Yuma, serving from 1887 to 1890. He enlisted in the army during the Spanish-American War and later served in China during the Boxer Rebellion. He died in Tucson in 1912.

In 1882, in a three-way race, Republican Jerome Ward beat out Carr and town Marshal Dave Neagle, who ran as an Independent. Ward's term was highlighted by the infamous Bisbee Massacre on December 8, 1883. On that evening five men robbed the Goldwater-Castaneda store and in the ensuing getaway, shot and killed four citizens, including a pregnant woman. The five men were apprehended, tried, convicted and sentenced to hang within a few months after the robbery-murders. A sixth man, John Heith, actually planned the robbery. He was tried separately from the others and given a prison sentence at the Yuma Territorial Prison. The citizens, including the town's leaders were so outraged they charged the county jail on the morning of February 22, took custody of Heith and lynched him to a telegraph pole on Tough Nut Street. Dr. George Goodfellow, the famous "Gunshot Physician" and county coroner, ruled the "deceased died of Emphysema of the lungs which might have been caused by strangulation self-inflicted or otherwise." A little more than a month later, on March 28, the five men were hanged in what was the largest mass hanging in Arizona history. Clearly the citizens of Cochise County had had enough of the lawlessness.

On July 6, 1900, Warren Earp, the youngest of the

fighting brothers, was shot and killed in a barroom fight in Willcox by a Cowboy named Johnny Boyette. Earp was unarmed but the jury ruled self-defense. Wyatt claimed it was murder.

Mattie Blaylock, Wyatt's "significant other" in Tombstone, went to the Earp family home in Colton for a time but when it became clear he wasn't coming back, headed back to Arizona and looked up her old friend, Big Nose Kate. Kate had opened a bordello in Globe after splitting up with Doc Holliday. Mattie eventually wound up in Pinal where she was found one July morning in 1888, dead from an overdose of laudanum and whiskey.

Big Nose Kate, whose real name was Mary Catherine Haroney, died in the Arizona Pioneers Home at Prescott in 1940. Photographs reveal a normal-size nose, so she might have earned her nickname from sticking her nose in everybody's business. Some might wonder how a woman like Big Nose Kate wound up in the respectable Pioneers Home. The late Prescott historian Budge Ruffner suggested that some Arizonans "gave their lives for honor but she gave her honor for life."

Wyatt and Virgil continued their restless wandering. For a time Virgil and Allie lived in Colton, California, where he served as town marshal, before moving to Vanderbilt, near the Arizona-Nevada border. A year later they moved to Cripple Creek, Colorado, where Virgil and Wyatt opened a saloon. In 1895, Virgil and Allie moved back to Prescott where he invested in a mine and worked as a deputy sheriff. San Diego was their next stop where he and Wyatt were involved in some business ventures.

While still a teenager, Virgil had married a girl named

Ellen Rysdam. Then, he'd gone off to fight in the Civil War. Somehow she believed he'd died in battle so she moved west to Oregon with her family. There, she gave birth to Virgil's child, a girl, Nellie Jane. Virgil also believed Ellen had died while he was away. Many years later the daughter, now grown, heard about the famous Virgil Earp and contacted him. In 1899, Virgil and Allie went to Portland where he was re-united with his ex-wife and daughter. It must have been a poignant, but joyful occasion for Virgil as he and Allie had no children.

The new boom town of Goldfield, Nevada, was the next residence for Virgil and Allie.

Virgil was still working as a lawman in 1905, when he died of pneumonia in Goldfield. His daughter Nellie Jane had the body buried at her hometown of Portland, Oregon. Two weeks after Virgil's death, the family patriarch, Nicholas Porter Earp, passed away in California. Allie Earp died in 1947.

After landing in Gunnison in 1882, Wyatt sent for Josie, who had gone home to San Francisco during the vendetta, to join him. The next year he led a group of "desperate men" to help his old friend Luke Short, in what became known as the "Dodge City War." The presence of several well-known gunfighters was enough to cause the other side to back down without a fight. A year later he and Josie headed for Eagle, Idaho, for a time, then it was off to Cripple Creek, Colorado. During the late 1890s, Wyatt involved himself in several entrepreneurial ventures including race horses, real estate, and his big love, gambling. In December, 1896, in San Francisco, he was asked to referee the heavyweight fight between Bob Fitzsimmons and Tom Sharkey. When Wyatt stepped into the ring and removed his coat, the crowd was somewhat astonished to see he was packing a Colt .45. Wyatt had been carrying a large amount of money and had forgotten to remove the revolver.

In the eighth round of the fight, Fitzsimmons sent Sharkey to the canvas with what looked like a knockout. Wyatt called a foul and ruled Sharkey the winner. The decision caused quite a furor. Wyatt was accused of betting heavily on Sharkey; however, a later investigation cleared Wyatt of any wrongdoing.

The following summer Wyatt and Josie left Yuma for San Francisco, on their way to the gold fields of Alaska. Gold had been discovered in the Klondike and they joined the rush of adventurers in search of pay dirt, opening a saloon in Nome. After two years in the "Land of the Midnight Sun," Wyatt pulled up stakes and cashed in, taking home some $85,000 in profits. In early 1902, they were back in business in the boom town of Tonopah, Nevada.

About this time Theodore Roosevelt was entertaining some of the old gunfighters when the president's press secretary, Stuart Lake, overheard Bat Masterson say something to the effect that the story of the true West would never be known until Wyatt Earp decided to tell his story. After Bat Masterson died in 1921, Lake decided it was time to go west and talk to Wyatt.

The result would be a classic book, *Wyatt Earp: Frontier Marshal.* Part truth and part fiction, this book would thrust Wyatt into legendary status.

Like the Old West, Tombstone itself was dying. The "Comstock of Arizona" had fallen on hard times. The mines started to flood in 1883. A few years later new pumps were installed, but a fire put them out of action and they were submerged. The labor movement was gaining momentum, along with the demonetization of silver, which caused many mining operations to shut down. The entrepreneurs and hardrock miners called it "deep enough" or quits and headed for new bonanzas. Things began to get quiet along notorious Allen Street. The sounds of laughter, clatter of the roulette wheel, shuffling of cards and the rinky-dink piano were about gone.

Tombstone, the great "Sagebrush Sodom," a city that rivaled the likes of New Orleans and San Francisco, was slowly fading like some worn out old vaudeville actor.

The Gunfight at the O.K. Corral might have been the defining moment of Wyatt Earp's life, but it says little about the total man. He spent a little more than two years in Tombstone and lived another 47 years after he left the "Town Too Tough To Die." Wyatt's life spanned 80 years, only six of which were spent as a lawman. His entire life was one of continuous adventure. He had an unquenchable thirst for gambling — high stakes, low stakes — anything as long as it was a game of chance. That's how he lived his life.

Wyatt Earp died peacefully in his sleep at 8:05 on the morning of January 13, 1929.

Josie had remained faithfully by his side for nearly 50 years. Since they had no children and most of his family was gone, she took his ashes home to San Francisco. She died in 1944 and rests beside him in a Jewish cemetery in Colma, a few miles south of San Francisco.

Wild Bill Smith:
A Cowboy Goes Bad

Perhaps not as publicized as the likes
of Johnny Ringo, John Wesley Hardin,
Billy the Kid, or Jesse James, Bill Smith and
his bunch could match any of their misdeeds.
Despite fierce efforts to capture him,
Smith got away and lapsed into obscurity.

A FEW YEARS AGO I WROTE A STORY FOR THE *ARIZONA Republic* newspaper about an outlaw named Bill Smith. Shortly thereafter I received a letter from one of his descendants thanking me for keeping the memory of Bill Smith alive. It wasn't too long ago that folks tried to disassociate themselves from outlaws in the family. Nowadays they point with pride to some rascal of an ancestor who a century ago was shunned by his relatives.

Around the turn of the century, the Bill Smith gang roamed the owl-hoot trails of Arizona and New Mexico as one of the wildest bands of desperados.

Captain Burton C. Mossman of the Arizona Rangers knew Smith about as well as anyone, and according to him the outlaw boss had once been an honest cowpuncher who had gone bad. According to Mossman, nobody seemed to know why Smith turned his back to the law. However, as we shall see, Bill Smith didn't spurn the chivalrous cowboy code of honor.

He stood about six feet tall with a slender, muscular frame, dark eyes and thick, coarse hair. The only flaw in his handsome features was a gap between his two front teeth. He was described as the kind of man who could arouse the interest of a "romantically inclined maiden."

Smith was about 35 years old when he turned outlaw. The ex-cowpuncher gathered around him a band that included two brothers, George and Al, along with four other hard-bitten border desperados.

A story is told that Bill Smith had drifted into the Oklahoma Territory in his younger days and ridden with the Dalton gang. He was back in Arizona by 1898. He was caught rustling cows in Navajo County and jailed in St. Johns. His younger brother, Al, was able to slip a pistol into the jail. One morning Bill appeared to be sleeping late when the jailer, Tom Berry, brought his breakfast. Berry leaned over to awaken the outlaw and found himself looking into a .44 Colt. Smith locked the jailer in his own cell and slipped out the back to a wood shed where Al had left a Winchester and some shells. Then he headed for New Mexico.

During the winter of 1900, the Bill Smith gang terrorized most of southwestern New Mexico, holding up travelers and robbing stores. The brazen outlaws raided ranches and rustled livestock in daylight. Their notoriety spread far and wide, and before long they were being accused of every killing and foul deed that occurred in the territory.

Finally, the citizens of southwest New Mexico grew weary of lawful efforts to apprehend the gang and formed a vigilance committee that numbered several hundred (New Mexico didn't have a territorial ranger force until 1905). The manhunters were in the saddle, constantly scouring the rugged country along the Arizona-New Mexico line. The relentless pressure soon drove the outlaws into Arizona, where they set up a base of operations in the remote Blue River country in northern Graham County. Bill and his brothers located at their mother's place. When word spread that the Smith gang was operating in eastern Arizona, Mossman dispatched four Rangers to the White Mountain area.

In early October, gang members were seen around Springerville. According to informants they had robbed a Union Pacific train in Utah. On the way back to their lair on the Blue River, they stole a bunch of horses from a rancher named Henry Barrett. Barrett organized a small posse and rode to Greer, where they joined up with Arizona Rangers Carlos Tafolla and Duane Hamblin.

Someone spotted the gang heading south near Springerville, and one of the Smith brothers was seen buying supplies in St. Johns.

The posse picked up the trail near Sheep Crossing, on the Little Colorado River, and followed it over to the Black River. At Lorenzo Crosby's ranch, they recruited three brothers, Crosby, Bill, and Arch Maxwell. The Maxwell brothers, from Nutrioso, were experienced trackers and had been friends with Bill Smith until he stole some livestock from them.

The posse followed the rustlers south past Big Lake and back to the Black River. An early winter storm had buried the White Mountains under a blanket of snow. On the afternoon of October 8, the posse heard three rifle shots and found patches of blood in the snow. The trail led toward a steep gorge.

Meanwhile, in a canyon near the headwaters of the Black River, Bill Smith and his gang made camp. They were skinning a bear one of them had shot late that after-noon when one of their bloodhounds picked up a scent and started howling. Bill climbed to the top of the rim for a look and saw riders coming. He charged back to camp and sounded the alarm.

The possemen picketed their horses some distance from the Smith camp and moved stealthily towards it. The Rangers, Tafolla and Hamblin, along with Bill Maxwell, headed out across a clearing while the other six took up positions on the edge of the rim. Barrett, the rancher, sized up the situation and called out for the possemen to take cover.

Hamblin dropped to the snow but Tafolla and Maxwell kept moving across the clearing. Soon the two found them-selves in the open in front of seven armed, desperate men not over forty feet away.

Arizona Ranger Harry Wheeler, during an interview years later with the *Tucson Citizen*, gave a romanticized account of the conversation between Bill Smith and the two lawmen:

"The two parties were now within forty feet of each other, Tafolla and Maxwell standing wholly unprotected by even a shrub, two dark spots against a snowy background of white. The outlaws were invisible except where each exposed a slight portion of his arm from behind the trunk of a great tree, supporting the protruding rifle barrels, which were now leveled at the two exposed men. There was silence for a few moments as the two gazed coolly and calmly into the mouths of seven guns beaded upon them. Maxwell was the first to break silence.

" 'Bill Smith,' he said, 'we arrest you in the name of the law and the territory of Arizona, and call upon you and your companions to lay down your arms.'

"By this time standing erect, their bodies straight and motionless, their minds still cool and calm and their voices without a tremor, the utter fearlessness of the two officers, now wholly at the mercy of the outlaws, must have touched a spark of gallantry in the outlaw chief to which we have already referred. In Tafolla he had recognized a former companion of his days on the ranch, where they had worked together upon the range. Calmly he addressed his words to that officer.

" 'Tafolla,' Smith said, 'we know each other pretty well, I believe. We have ridden the range together in times past in better days than these — better than any which can ever come into my life again. We have spent many an hour of weary toil and hardships upon the plains and we have enjoyed many pleasures together. I liked you then and I like you still. For your own sake, for the sake of your wife and your babies, I would spare you now. I would also spare your companion. Go your way Tafolla. Give me the benefit of one day and I will leave here and never trouble this country again. But do not try to take me, for, by God, I will never be taken — neither I nor any member of my party. Your decision must be made immediately for it is getting dark.' "

Wheeler continued his account saying that in replying to Smith "there was not the slightest deviation in the tone of Tafolla's voice from that used in demanding the surrender ... If anything, he spoke more slowly and more calmly than he did in the first instance.

" 'Bill, this friendship between you and me is a thing of the past. As for offering to spare our lives, we may thank you for that and no more. For thirty days we've followed you, half-starved and half-frozen. Now we stand together or fall together. The only request I have to make of you — and I make that for old time's sake — is that if Maxwell and I shall forfeit our lives here, you will send to Captain Mossman the news and manner of our death.

" 'Let him know that neither he nor the other members of the force need feel ashamed of the manner in which we laid down our lives on this spot this day. There is no more to be said; Bill, merely remember that a Ranger is speaking, and command you for the last time to surrender.'

"There was a brief fusillade of shots and all was over. The forms of Ranger Tafolla and Deputy Sheriff Maxwell lay huddled together in the snow. The men lived long enough to fight their rifles empty, for Smith — for some reason perhaps he could not have analyzed himself — evidently strove to spare the men's lives, who so willingly died in trying to take his life. Dead shot that he was, he had placed three bullets in the hat of each man, just above the scalp, hoping, no doubt, that he would frighten the men into retreat without his having to kill them. But finding that he was dealing with men who had no fear of death, and having himself finally received a wound in his foot, he reluctantly lowered the range of his rifle."

Harry Wheeler, last captain of the Arizona Rangers, told the *Tucson Citizen* in 1907 he had gathered the information from "Captain Mossman and others connected with the fight and pursuit."

Part of Wheeler's story doesn't jibe with other accounts. It's hard to say what really happened in those frenzied moments before the fight.

Henry Barrett's account of the battle saw it a little differently.

According to Barrett, Maxwell called for the gang to surrender:

"All right," Bill Smith replied. "Which way do you want us to come out?"

"Come right out this way," Maxwell ordered.

Bill Smith walked boldly into the clearing, dragging his rifle, a new .303 Savage, behind him to cleverly conceal it from the lawmen.

When he was about forty feet away, Smith jumped behind a tree, raised his rifle, and fired a round, hitting Tafolla in the belly. Yet, he kept firing his Winchester until he was out of shells.

Smith's rifle blazed again, hitting Maxwell in the head.

The fighting became general. A furious fusillade of gunfire echoed over that snowy basin. The rest of the posse opened fire from the rim. Smith dove for cover and returned fire with his men from behind trees.

Hamblin was able slip around to where the outlaws had picketed their horses. He turned loose nine saddle horses and a pack mule, leaving the gang afoot. The posse poured a withering fire down on the rustlers forcing them to retreat into the thick woods as night fell. Smith and one other outlaw had been wounded.

When the smoke lifted and the outlaws had fled, the posse moved in. Maxwell lay dead in the snow. Tafolla, hit twice in the belly, lay mortally wounded, begging for water. He would live in agony for several more hours.

The little clearing would be known henceforth as Battle Ground.

It was said that Bill Maxwell's bullet-riddled hat remained at Battle Ground clearing for sometime afterward as the superstitious cowboys riding through the area refused to go near it.

Captain Mossman was at Solomonville when word arrived of the deaths of the two brave lawmen. He organized a posse and recruited two Apache trackers from San Carlos — Old Josh and Chicken.

The outlaws made their way to a cow camp on Beaver Creek. There, cowpunchers told them Bill Maxwell had been killed in the clearing. Smith claimed to be remorseful at learning this.

"Well, I'm sure, sure sorry," he said, "When he stood up that way we thought it was Barrett. He was the one we wanted. We feel mighty sorry over killing Bill Maxwell. He was a good friend of ours. Tell Bill's mother for us that we're very sorry we killed him."

Bill Smith and his gang headed for Bear Valley, east of the Blue River. They rode into Hugh McKean's ranch at supper time and tried to buy some horses. Bill pulled out a roll of bills but McKean wouldn't sell. So, at gun point the gang took his horses, saddles, guns, and a sack of grub and headed for New Mexico. Again, Smith said he was sorry he had killed Bill Maxwell but was glad he had killed a Ranger.

Mossman's Apache trackers followed the trail to the McKean ranch, arriving a day after the outlaws had ridden east. Mossman and his Rangers kept up the chase until they were driven back to McKean's ranch by another snow storm. When the weather broke, the Apaches picked up the trail again.

Mossman stubbornly continued the chase all the way to the Rio Grande before losing the trail for good near Socorro, New Mexico.

The Arizona Rangers' persistence paid off. The Bill

Smith gang was driven out of Arizona. Smith's mother later told a Ranger that Bill and Al had gone to Galveston, Texas, and taken a boat for Argentina. Several years later, George turned himself in to Graham County Sheriff Jim Parks. The only charges against him were in Apache County, so he was turned loose. He went back to live on his mother's ranch.

The rest of Bill Smith's life remains a puzzle. Frazier Hunt, Mossman's biographer, said that Smith shot Ranger Dayton Graham in Douglas. Graham later hunted down and killed the outlaw.

But the person Graham killed probably was not Bill Smith.

Did Bill Smith stay in Argentina or did he return and assume a new identity? If his mother knew, she never told.

Hunt also wrote that Bill Smith later sent a letter to Mossman detailing those last moments in the lives of lawmen Tafolla and Maxwell. If that's true, then despite the fact that Bill Smith became one of the most ruthless desperados of his time, he followed a code of honor that bonded those men of the breed.

CHAPTER FIVE

Burt Mossman: A Cattleman Runs the Arizona Rangers

Around the turn of the century, vicious bands of outlaws sullied Arizona's reputation as it strived to gain statehood. One measure to whip the bandits and further statehood efforts was the formation of the Arizona Rangers. Their first leader was an Illinois native who began working as a cowhand when he was 15.

———

ARIZONA GREETED THE 20TH CENTURY AS A FRONTIER Jekyll and Hyde. On one hand, communities such as Phoenix, Prescott, and Tucson were becoming modern cities. Churches and schools outnumbered the bawdy houses and saloons, a sure sign that civilization was making progress. On the other hand, the rural, mountainous regions still provided a refuge for desperados. Large bands of outlaws holed up in the primitive wilderness of northeastern Arizona's White Mountains. Mexico was a sanctuary for border bandits.

In Arizona, outlaws on the run in other territories and states could find a haven in the labyrinth of canyons and brooding mountains where there were few towns and roads, which mostly were cattle trails.

With the completion of the Santa Fe line on the north

and the Southern Pacific on the south, stagecoach robbers turned to a new line of work. Between 1897 and 1900 there were six train robberies on the Southern Pacific alone. Bands of rustlers boldly stole cattle in broad daylight, driving small outfits out of business. Payrolls for the mines were being robbed regularly.

During the 1880s there was a large outcry from ranching and mining interests for a territorial police similar to the famous Texas Rangers. By the turn of the century, politicians were trying to convince the U.S. Congress that Arizona was ready for statehood. However, many members of Congress thought Arizona should not be admitted until it quelled lawlessness.

In March, 1901, Arizona raised a quasi-military company patterned after the Texas Rangers. Initially, the Arizona Rangers consisted of 14 men, including a captain and a sergeant, who could shoot straight and fast and ride hard and long. A ranger's term of enlistment was one year; the captain would receive $125 a month, the sergeant $75, and the 12 privates would be paid $55 a month.

Each man had to furnish his own rifle, pistol, and horse. But the politicians allowed each ranger $1.50 to feed himself and his horse. Funding for the ranger force would come from a territory-wide tax.

Officially, the Arizona Rangers' duties were to assist local law enforcement agencies, prevent train robberies, and run the rustlers out of the territory.

They were placed under the command of the governor, an arrangement that created problems. Territorial governors were appointed from Washington, while legislators were elected locally. Most governors were Republicans but Democrats controlled the Legislature. Thus, many legislators viewed the Rangers as the governor's private police force.

The territory-wide tax posed another problem. The rangers were most needed in the rural counties in the mountains or near the Mexican border, so counties such as the populous Maricopa County had little need for the free-ranging lawmen and resented having to share the tax burden.

Local lawmen became jealous of the colorful rangers, whose activities were followed closely by an adoring press. Local lawmen shared the dangers with rangers but found themselves left out of the newspaper stories and became resentful.

Burton C. Mossman was Governor Nathan O. Murphy's choice to be captain of the Arizona Rangers. The rawhide-tough cowman had made quite a reputation for himself when he ran the famous Hashknife outfit in northern Arizona.

The son of a Civil War hero, Mossman was a descendant of the Scots-Irish, an intractable, hell-for-leather people who carved out a niche of history on the American frontier a century earlier. At 5 feet 10 inches tall and 180 pounds, he was stocky and broad-shouldered. Born in Illinois, Mossman was drawing a cowboy's pay in New Mexico by the time he was fifteen.

He quickly earned a reputation as quick-tempered, wild, and restless. But he was dependable and honest, earning him the respect of the ranchers for whom he worked. Once he walked 110 miles across a dry, burning desert to deliver an important letter for his boss. He made the 47-hour journey on foot because he thought it was too dry to take a horse.

By the time he was 21, Mossman was foreman of a ranch in New Mexico that ran 8,000 head of cattle. At 27, he was managing a big outfit in the Bloody Basin in Arizona's rugged central mountains. Three years later he was named superintendent for the troubled Aztec Land and Cattle Company, better-known as the Hashknife outfit.

The fabled Hashknife ranch, one of the biggest cattle operations in the West, was on the verge of

BURT MOSSMAN

bankruptcy when Mossman was called in to keep it from going belly-up.

The Eastern-owned outfit had been running as many as 60,000 head of beef over two million acres. Gangs of rustlers, some employed by the company, had pushed the ranch to near-bankruptcy. The ranch had been frustrated in its attempts to stop the rustling because area residents resented the large, absentee ownership that — because of land grants — was able to graze cattle free on the public domain. Consequently, local juries were prone to find defendants not guilty. Also, rustlers sometimes were able to get a friend on the jury to disrupt things, causing a mistrial or hung jury. In fourteen years of trying, the Hashknife hadn't been able to get a single conviction.

Burt Mossman got right into his new job. On his first

day the scrappy cowman captured three rustlers. Then he fired 52 of the 84 cowboys on the Hashknife payroll and installed trusted cowmen as wagon bosses. He visited local leaders and convinced them to take a stand against cattle rustlers. Soon, he had the outfit turning a profit again.

But, Mossman couldn't control the weather, the cowman's greatest nemesis. A prolonged drought, followed by a calamitous blizzard, finished off the company in 1901.

Despite the failure of the Hashknife, Mossman earned a reputation as a formidable foe of cattle rustlers and a savvy businessman. He located in Bisbee, where he opened a beef market with Ed Toverea. But he didn't stay in that business long.

When the Arizona Rangers force was organized, Governor Murphy wanted a special kind of hombre to manage more than a dozen high-spirited lawmen. His choice, Burt Mossman, agreed to a one-year enlistment, during which the Rangers achieved some of their greatest success before being disbanded in 1909.

He located the Ranger headquarters in Bisbee and set about recruiting his force. The task wasn't hard. Every young man in the territory with a spirit of adventure wanted to ride with Mossman's Rangers.

He selected his men carefully, dressed them as working cowboys, and had them hire out to outfits where rustling had been a problem. Operating undercover, they infiltrated cliques of rustlers. They kept their badges concealed and pinned them only when an arrest was imminent.

The Rangers met their greatest challenge early on when they took on the notorious Bill Smith gang. Run out of New Mexico, the gang had set up operations at Smith's

widowed mother's place near Harpers Mill on the Blue
River.

Taking on Bill Smith and his renegade band turned
into a sad and disappointing experience for the new force.
Bill Smith gunned down Ranger Carlos Tafolla and Apache
County Deputy Sheriff Bill Maxwell near the headwaters of
the Black River in eastern Arizona. Mossman was determined to run the gang into the ground. He chased the outlaws all the way to the Rio Grande but never got Bill Smith.
The only satisfaction for Mossman was that the gang was
driven out of Arizona for good.

Next, the Rangers went after the Musgrove gang, led
by George Musgrove and his brother, Canley. They were
wanted in Texas and New Mexico for robbery and murder.
The Musgroves also had ridden with the Black Jack gang, a
tempestuous band of highwaymen who had ravaged along
the Arizona-New Mexico border.

The successful raid on the Musgroves came after lawmen learned that one of the gang, Witt Neill, had a girlfriend
living on the Blue River. Then, Deputy Sheriff John Parks
received a tip that several well-armed, suspicious-looking
men were seen at the mouth of the Blue River, north of
Clifton. He passed the information on to Graham County
Sheriff Jim Parks at Solomonville, and to Captain Mossman at
Bisbee. Parks and Mossman rushed to Clifton and organized
a posse to go after the marauders. They headed for the girlfriend's place. Arriving late at night, the lawmen surrounded
the cabin and waited for dawn. At first light they closed in
and found Neill sleeping on the porch. He awoke looking into
the muzzles of several pistols and rifles. Although the
rustler had a Winchester rifle and a pair of six-guns tucked
under the covers, he wisely surrendered without a fight.

Two other members of the gang, George Cook and Joe Roberts, were spotted that same day driving some stolen horses. The two were believed to have robbed a store in New Mexico, murdering the owner. And they fit the description of two men who had robbed a postal office at Fort Sumner the previous January.

The posse split up and surrounded the men without being spotted. The unwary rustlers were apprehended and hustled off to the jail at Solomonville.

With that capture and a couple of others, the Musgrove gang was shattered and remaining members scattered.

Cooperation between the Rangers and the Mexican police generally was good. The Mexican force, called *Rurales*, were sternly led by Emilio Kosterlitzsky, one of the most remarkable men in the border country. A Russian by birth, he spoke several languages fluently and was a man of great intellect. He came to Mexico as a young man and joined the ranks of the *Rurales* as a private. He rose to the rank of colonel in President Porfirio Diaz's feared police.

The *Rurales* operated under the law of *ley fugar,* or "law of flight." In other words, they brought in few live prisoners. The common practice was to say the captive was "shot while trying to escape." It was a brutal, but effective, way of lowering the population of the border bandits.

The Rangers and Kosterlitzsky didn't bother with the legal formalities when dealing with fugitives. Kosterlitzsky had appointed the Rangers as officers in his force, allowing them to cross the border in pursuit of fugitives.

A wanted man in Arizona might be sitting in a cantina in Cananea thinking he was safe. He might go upstairs with some pretty *señorita* to have a nightcap and the next thing he realized, he was in the Bisbee jail. How did he get there?

His lady friend was working with the Rangers. She had slipped him a mickey — a knockout drug — and handed him over to the *Rurales*, who, in turn, hauled him to the border with a gunny sack over his head and turned him over to the Rangers. Mossman's men learned early on that the best source of information came from the ubiquitous saloon girls in the border towns.

One night near the end of Mossman's enlistment, he was involved in a fracas at the Orient Saloon in Bisbee. He and Ranger Bert Grover were sitting in a poker game with some $400 in the pot, which was won by a local gambler. Grover accused the gambler of cheating and jerked his six-shooter. Mossman tried to calm Grover just as a couple of Bisbee police officers arrived. When the policemen arrested Grover, Mossman and another Ranger, Leonard Page, joined in a donnybrook that wound up in the street in front of the Orient, much to the delight of the Saturday night revelers of Brewery Gulch. Grover finally was placed under arrest and taken to jail. A few hours later the resourceful Page purloined the keys to the jail and freed his comrade.

The citizens of Bisbee were upset by the Rangers' rowdy actions and 200 of them signed a petition demanding that Governor Murphy relieve Mossman of his command. Most of those signing the petition, however, were barflies, tin horns, and other wretches with an ax to grind. A group of respectable citizens circulated another petition in support of Mossman.

A couple of days later, Mossman submitted his

resignation to the governor. He hadn't planned to stay in the low-paying position long when he signed on. Besides, his good friend Governor Murphy was leaving office and Mossman might have felt it was time to move on. Also, he was a typical cowhand, free and independent, and the incident in Bisbee might have soured him on public service.

During Burt Mossman's tour of duty, the Rangers put 125 men behind bars. Remarkably, considering the kinds of hard-bitten desperados they were dealing with, the Rangers killed only one man. The only Ranger killed in the line was duty was Carlos Tafolla.

While Captain Mossman was waiting for his resignation to become effective, he needed to tie up some loose ends. During the past year he had become obsessed with capturing Augustine Chácon, one of the most cunning and rapacious outlaws in the border country. Chácon lived in the Mexican state of Sonora but made periodic forays into Arizona. In a boast to a law officer, the handsome *bandito* claimed that he had killed 37 Mexicans and 15 Americans. He was looked upon in Sonora and among the Mexicans working in the mining camps of Arizona as a folk hero because he had given the *gringo* lawmen such fits. But, in reality, he was a diabolical killer.

During the robbery of a store in Morenci on Christmas Eve, 1895, he slit the throat of the shopkeeper with a hunting knife. A posse cornered him and tried to negotiate a surrender. During the parley, he shot posseman Pablo Salcito.

Salcito, who was acquainted with the outlaw, had tied a white handkerchief to the barrel of his rifle and had walked to within a few feet of Chácon when the outlaw gunned him down. In the ensuing gun battle, Chácon was wounded and captured. A jury in Graham County sentenced him to hang.

Chácon escaped the hangman's noose in Solomonville by breaking out of jail nine days before his sentence was to be carried out. His inamorata in Solomonville had slipped him a file concealed in the spine of a Bible. Members of a mariachi band were doing time for some transgression so Chácon had them play a cacophony of *corridos* to drown the noise while he sawed through the bars.

Chácon's pretty girlfriend had flirted with the jailer on several occasions and on the night of the escape she persuaded the unwitting fellow to take her for a midnight stroll. The obliging jailer returned later to find his prisoner had fled. On his way to Sonora, Chácon murdered two prospectors. He managed to evade both Mexican and American lawmen for the next five years.

Burt Mossman made up his mind that the capture of Augustine Chácon would be his crowning glory as Ranger captain. He concocted a daring plan to slip into Sonora, pose as an outlaw on the run, and gain the outlaw's confidence long enough to take him prisoner. But he would need some accomplices. He found them in two homesick *gringo* fugitives, Burt Alvord and Billy Stiles.

Alvord had been a lawman at Willcox but decided to up his economic station by moonlighting outside the law. He wasn't considered too bright so he figured he would never be suspected of masterminding train robberies. To pull the train heists, Alvord recruited several reprobates, including "Three-Fingered" Jack Dunlap, "Bravo Juan" Yoas, and Billy Stiles. They succeeded admirably on the first, robbing some $30,000 from the Southern Pacific near Cochise on September 11, 1899. Lawman Bert Grover, who would later serve in the Rangers, strongly suspected Alvord but didn't have enough evidence to make an arrest.

Caught up in their success, the gang tried to rob the train station in Fairbank on February 15, 1900. The outlaws didn't figure on legendary lawman

BURT ALVORD

Jeff Milton riding shotgun that day. When the smoke cleared, the outlaws rode away empty-handed. A robber known as "Bravo Juan" had a load of buckshot in his rear and "Three-Fingered" Jack was mortally wounded. The outlaws abandoned Jack along the trail and when the posse caught up he gave a death-bed confession. Burt Alvord and what was left of his gang high-tailed it for Sonora.

Two years later, Burt Mossman heard that Alvord and Stiles wanted to come home. In January, 1902, he got word to the fugitives that if they would help him capture Chácon, they could share the reward money and he would testify in court to their good character. He even went so far as to put Billy Stiles on the payroll as a Ranger. Alvord's wife was threatening to divorce him if he didn't come home soon. That gave Mossman some added leverage.

Apparently, Colonel Emilio Kosterlitzsky knew of

Mossman's plans to make the illegal capture of a Mexican citizen but had no plans to interfere as long as the Ranger didn't create a situation that would force him to get involved. He, too, wanted Chácon brought to justice.

Burt Mossman rode into Mexico in September, 1902, posing as a fugitive. He learned Alvord was holed up west of the village of San Jose de Pima. Two days later he rode into the lair of the lawman-turned-outlaw. The hilltop adobe house was a fortress with loopholes, battle shutters on the doors and windows, and a commanding view of the surrounding terrain. Inside, horses were saddled and ready to ride.

Alvord spent some time thinking about Mossman's offer. He missed his wife and wanted to go home but didn't want to betray Chácon. Finally, he agreed to cooperate. Mossman then rode north to await word from Alvord on where he could meet Chácon. Billy Stiles would be the messenger.

A few days later, Billy Stiles brought word that he, Mossman and Alvord would meet Chácon at a spring 16 miles south of the border. To entice Chácon out in the open, they offered to cut him in on a plan to steal some prize horses from the ranch of Colonel William C. Greene in Arizona's San Rafael Valley.

Mossman and Stiles rode to the spring, but Alvord and Chácon failed to show. They rode back across the border to spend the night, then returned the next day. Around sunset the following day they met the two outlaws on the trail. Both were armed heavily. Along with his rifle and pistol, Chácon was packing a large knife. Despite assurances by Mossman, claiming that he too was a fugitive, the cagey bandit was suspicious. His hand was never far from the butt of his six-gun.

That night they made camp, and Mossman nervously waited out sleepless hours, his coat pulled up, concealing his face. Beneath the coat, his pistol was trained on Chácon. The ever-vigilant Chácon refused to let any of the men get behind him. To make matters worse, Mossman wasn't sure he could trust either Alvord or Stiles not to betray him.

At daybreak, the men got up and started a fire. While Chácon was fixing breakfast, Alvord slipped next to Mossman and quietly said he had done his part and was heading out. He also warned the Ranger not to trust Billy Stiles. Then he told Chácon he was going for water and would return shortly. While the three men were eating, Chácon's eyes narrowed, and he wondered what was taking Alvord so long to return.

After breakfast, Chácon reached in his pocket and took out some corn husk cigarettes and offered them to Stiles and Mossman. As they hunkered down around the fire having a smoke, Mossman saw his chance. He let his cigarette go out, then reached into the fire with his right hand, picked up a burning stick and re-lit his cigarette. As he reached out and tossed the stick back into the fire Mossman's hand slid past his holster. Quick as a flash, the Ranger pulled his revolver and got the drop on the surprised bandit. He ordered Chácon to put his hands up. The outlaw cursed but did as he was told. Next, the Ranger told Stiles to remove Chácon's knife and gunbelt. And, to Billy's surprise, told him to drop his gunbelt also. He then ordered both men to step back while he gathered in the rifles and pistols. After ordering Stiles to handcuff Chácon, the three mounted up and rode for the border.

THE HANGING OF AUGUSTINE CHÁCON

Mossman decided to avoid Naco, fearing Chácon might have friends there. Instead, he headed across the San Pedro Valley about ten miles west. Stiles rode in front, leading Chácon's horse while Mossman covered them both from the rear with his Winchester 30-.40. As they neared the border, Chácon began to balk. So, Mossman unstrapped his riata and dropped a loop around Chácon's neck, warning that he would drag him across the border if necessary. The outlaw cursed again but caused no more trouble.

They arrived at Packard Station on the El Paso and Southwestern Railroad line just as the train to Benson was passing through. Mossman's luck was holding. He flagged it down and they made the final fifty miles to Benson riding the steel rails. At Benson, they were met by Graham County Sheriff Jim Parks, who was most eager to take

Chácon back to the jail at Solomonville and his long-awaited rendezvous with the hangman.

At 1 P.M. on November 21, 1902, Augustine Chácon climbed the thirteen steps to the top of the scaffold and gave a thirty minute speech that would have done a politician proud, closing with, "It's too late now, time to hang ... *Adios, todos amigos!*"

Thus ended the career of one of Arizona's most notorious outlaws.

Word of Mossman's daring capture caused a lot of excitement around the territory. It also raised outcries because his Ranger commission had expired four days before he captured Chácon and he had arrested the bandit in Mexico. The Mexican government expressed outrage at the flagrant violation of their sovereign soil. Mossman stayed around Arizona just long enough to keep his promise to Billy Stiles. After testifying for Billy he boarded a train and headed for New York City where he was greeted royally by a grateful Colonel Bill Greene. He spent the next few weeks far removed from the political rumpus he had created in Arizona.

Eventually, Mossman went back to New Mexico, where he became a successful rancher. He died in Roswell in 1956. A few years later he was inducted into the National Cowboy Hall of Fame in Oklahoma City. Chiseled out of old granite, Mossman was one of the truly great cattlemen and lawmen of the Old West.

Buckey O'Neill: Capturing The Canyon Diablo Robbers

History, romantic folklore, and bizarre
coincidences mix together to make
this tale. Years after a train robbery, legendary
Sheriff Buckey O'Neill and one of the bandits
he caught died on the same battlefield,
fighting for the same cause.

━━━⋙⋅⋘━━━

ANYON DIABLO WAS JUST A COLLECTION OF WOODEN shacks, tents, and sandstone buildings alongside a 256-feet-deep chasm between Flagstaff and Winslow in northern Arizona. The town had a short life, lasting some ten years. It boomed in the early 1880s during construction of a wooden trestle across the canyon for the Atlantic and Pacific Railroad, later called the Atcheson, Topeka and Santa Fe or just the Santa Fe.

It's said that more people were killed in Canyon Diablo in 1881-1882 than in Dodge City, Abilene, and Tombstone combined. All were men except for a prostitute whose throat was cut. Hell Street was the main drag and the main businesses included 14 saloons, 10 gambling casinos, two dance halls, and four houses of prostitution. The two favorite and most prominent madams were B.S. Mary (B.S. stands for what you think it does), and

Clabberfoot Mary, who had an hourglass figure and no problems with her feet.

Since the town had no newspaper, little of its history was recorded. A few stories have been handed down and have become a part of the local lore. One concerned a payroll robbery.

The enraged track layers and gandy dancers formed a posse and took out after the robber. As he was being chased, the robber lost his saddlebags containing the loot.

The posse caught the outlaw and decided to hang him on the spot. Someone threw a rope over a tree limb. But on this day the bandit was lucky. Lightning struck the tree. The posse believed the strike signaled divine intervention and decided to turn the man over to the proper authorities.

Several years later a cowboy happened upon some weather-beaten saddlebags half-buried in the sagebrush south of Canyon Diablo. Unfortunately the greenbacks were weathered beyond repair.

Canyon Diablo figured into another bizarre event. It began on the evening of Saturday, April 8, 1905, when cowhands John Shaw and Bill Smith bellied up to the bar in the Wigwam Saloon in Winslow and ordered whiskey. The drinks were set up but the pair was distracted by stacks of silver dollars at a dice game. On impulse, the pair drew their six-guns and pulled a heist.

Having filled their pockets with silver, they backed into the street, leaving their drinks and a trail of dropped dollars. Lawmen picked up the trail of money and followed it to the railroad tracks, where the pair had jumped aboard a slow-moving freight train westbound for Flagstaff. Lawmen in Flagstaff were notified and the two groups closed in, hoping to catch the pair at Canyon Diablo.

There, two lawmen confronted the robbers. Faced off about six feet apart, the four men fired 21 shots. The officers were unhurt. Smith was seriously wounded. Shaw was killed and buried in a pine box at Canyon Diablo.

The next night at the Wigwam, someone pointed out the two outlaws hadn't finished their drinks. One thing led to another and the boys decided unfortunate Shaw had paid for his drink and should have a chance to drink it. "Poor devil had gone to his grave thirsty," some barfly lamented.

Well, the boys decided to remedy the situation. About 15 boisterous cowhands boarded the westbound to Canyon Diablo. Upon arriving, they borrowed shovels and dug up the outlaw. Strangely, his death mask bore a faint grin. While the boys propped up Shaw's carcass and poured a drink down his guzzle, the macabre event was recorded with a Kodak box camera. Apparently the sight of the grinning corpse had a sobering affect on the revelers for after covering it up again, they all joined in to sing *Bringing in the Sheaves*.

Another story concerns a train robbery pulled in 1889 and Yavapai County Sheriff William O. "Buckey" O'Neill.

Buckey O'Neill was one of the most remarkable characters to ride in the cavalcade of Arizona history. He earned his nickname from his inclination to "buck the tiger" or bet against the house in faro. A dashing figure, he stood about six feet tall, had dark brown hair, and a stylish mustache. Women loved his handsome looks, infectious smile, and wit. He had a vibrant, magnetic personality that inspired loyalty and devotion from men and women alike.

He also had a strong sense of justice and would fight readily for a just cause. And, as the four who pulled the

1889 train robbery would learn, he had the tenacity of a bulldog.

Buckey O'Neill was only 19 when he rode into Phoenix on a burro in 1879. He was a printer or typesetter.

Tombstone, the silver boom town, lured him. There, he frequented the gambling halls along Allen Street, mixing with the likes of Wyatt Earp, Doc Holliday, Bat Masterson, Luke Short, and "Buckskin Frank" Leslie. For a time he was a reporter for John Clum's *Tombstone Epitaph*.

In 1882 he returned to Phoenix, where he worked as a deputy for noted Phoenix lawman Henry Garfias. It was here that O'Neill got his baptism of fire when three drunken cowboys rode down Washington Street firing pistols.

One of the men, Bill Hardy, rode his horse through the swinging doors of the Tiger Saloon and banged his head on the chandelier. Angrily, he fired several shots into the ceiling before riding back into the street. As Garfias, O'Neill, and two other officers rode slowly towards the trio, Hardy yelled, "Boys, here they come! Let's meet them."

Then he rode hell-for-leather towards the lawmen, shouting, "Come on you sons of bitches!"

As Hardy fired wildly, Garfias calmly slid out of the saddle and took aim. His first shot slammed into Hardy's pistol hand. The second emptied Hardy's saddle with a mortal wound. That took the starch out of the other two, and they surrendered.

Soon after the shoot-out, O'Neill went to work for the Prescott *Miner*. In 1885, he started a small livestock newspaper, the *Hoof and Horn.* He cut a colorful swath along "Whiskey Row," made friends easily, and liked politics. In 1886, he was elected probate judge. Two years later he was elected sheriff of Yavapai County. O'Neill had been in office just three months when the sensational train robbery at Canyon Diablo occurred.

It seemed that for case-hardened Hashknife cowpunchers Dan Harvick, Jack J. Smith, Bill Sterin, and John Halford the northern Arizona winter of 1888-89 would never end. Day after day they gazed across that wind-swept plateau impatiently waiting for spring roundup. Like it did to most cowhands, the winter hibernation and riding the grub line made them surly. They all were broke and reduced to playing cards with dried up beans for money.

With life so tedious, Harvick began to think of easier and more exciting ways of making money. He came up with a plan to rob a train. He shared his plan with the other three, then quietly drew his pay and rode out.

He camped that night in Box Canyon with the wind howling and blowing freezing sleet. Next morning, huddled over a small fire, he watched a lone rider approach. He nodded stiffly as J.J. Smith came riding in. In a couple of days, as expected, Sterin and Halford also appeared.

The four desperados spent the next few hours huddled around a blazing fire, their backsides to the bitter cold and made plans to rob the eastbound Santa Fe at Canyon Diablo two days hence. To cover their trail, they would ride south towards the Mogollon Rim, turn west, and then circle around to the north. Along the way, they made a costly mistake by burglarizing Will Barnes' ranch at the mouth of Box Canyon, where the Chevelon River forks with the Little Colorado River.

Barnes and his friend Bill Broadbent picked up the trail and followed the tracks toward Winslow. Just outside of town, the tracks veered west toward Sunset Pass. The

HASHKNIFE COWBOYS POSE IN HOLBROOK

two cowpunchers knew they couldn't follow the trail in the dark, so they rode into Winslow for the night.

Meanwhile, the outlaws picked their way through the rocks and brush until they reached the steel rails of the Santa Fe's main line. The four men followed the tracks until they caught the orange glow of a lamp in the window of the tiny train station. They reined in their horses, dismounted, built a small fire, and waited for the train.

That night, March 20, 1889, engineer Charles Wood eased the Santa Fe Eastbound No. 2 across the spindly trestle over Canyon Diablo. The train was but a short distance from the station at Canyon Diablo where the crew would take on water and fill up the wood box before going on to Winslow, 25 miles away. Wood stared at the face of his pocket watch. It was a few minutes before eleven.

At eleven o'clock sharp, Wood throttled down the locomotive at the Canyon Diablo station. The fireman, lantern in hand, climbed down the ladder. A light snow was falling, turning the ground white. From the darkness, a voice ordered him to lift his arms. He looked up to see two men, their faces masked with neckerchiefs, pointing pistols at his chest. A moment later he saw three men walking towards him. The one in the middle was engineer Wood. Two grizzled, hard-looking men carrying six-guns walked on either side of him.

The masked bandits led the two trainmen to the express car and threatened to blow it up with dynamite if the messenger inside refused to open the door. The fireman pounded on the door and identified himself. They heard the bolt slide back. The door opened, and messenger E.G. Knickerbocker stuck his head out. A step away from him was a Wells Fargo sawed-off shotgun, but the messenger wisely surrendered.

The outlaws fired several warning shots to keep the curious passengers from leaving their cars. And, just for devilment, one bandit fired a shot into the wall of the station house, sending the agent scurrying for cover.

J.J. Smith and Dan Harvick climbed into the car and ordered the messenger to open the safe. Knickerbocker claimed it was on a time lock set by Santa Fe officials and he couldn't open it. Smith then motioned with his pistol towards the Wells Fargo box and told Knickerbocker to empty its contents.

The two outlaws stuffed their pockets with valuables and rejoined Stiren and Halford, who still were holding their guns on the fireman and engineer. The bandits forced the two trainmen to walk with them to where their horses were picketed. After the four bandits were mounted, they let the trainmen go. A few minutes later, the locomotive was racing toward Winslow with its whistle blowing.

Snow continued to fall as the four train robbers rode south a few miles, then halted to build a fire and divvy up the spoils. The loot came to about $7,000 in cash along with some jewelry. Any jewelry that might be recognized was buried to be retrieved later. (The jewelry was never recovered and likely remains where it was cached.)

Smith's share of the loot included a pair of diamond earrings. He took the diamonds out of their settings and put them in his pocket. Later he reached in for some tobacco dregs to fill his pipe and accidentally dropped in the diamonds too. Later, he knocked the ashes out of the pipe bowl on his boot heel and the diamonds were lost.

In Winslow, Will Barnes had gone to the railroad station and telegraphed authorities in Holbrook about the burglary at his ranch. Then, he and Broadbent headed for a local hotel to get some sleep before resuming the chase. About midnight they were awakened by the dispatcher who told them about the train robbery.

Barnes and Broadbent loaded their horses on a stock car and headed for Canyon Diablo. On arriving, they found horse tracks that matched the ones at the ranch. One of the horses had been shod with the toe out of line. Another had three nails on the inside of the shoe, instead of the usual four. Still another had been shod with a second-hand shoe, causing the nail heads to protrude.

From the descriptions and prints, Barnes was pretty sure he knew the identities of two of the train robbers.

He and Broadbent found the spot where the outlaws had stopped to divide the loot. Barnes found some torn Wells Fargo envelopes, a five-dollar gold piece, and silver coins that the robbers had evidently lost in their haste.

The bandits tried to cover their tracks with a variety of means. They tied bits of saddle blankets to their horses' hooves. They fell in with a herd of wild, range mares and drove them for a distance. And, they rode through dry, rocky washes. But, the two stubborn trackers kept cutting trail until they picked up the shod tracks again.

Barnes and Broadbent followed the outlaws' trail south for several miles before it bent around to the north and crossed the railroad tracks about fifteen miles west of Winslow. By this time their horses were about played out. Barnes suspected the train robbers were headed for Lees Ferry on the Colorado River.

The two trackers rode on to Lees Ferry, where they were disappointed to be told the outlaws had not crossed the river at that point. But the fugitives had crossed without the ferry boat operator seeing them. They had bribed a man to cross on the ferry and camp for the night. Then, when the ferryman went to sleep, the man stole the boat and brought the desperados and their horses across under cover of darkness.

At Lees Ferry, Barnes and Broadbent were met by Sheriff O'Neill and a posse from Prescott. The two weary cowmen then rode back to Holbrook.

O'Neill and Deputy Jim Black were in Flagstaff when word came of the train robbery. They were joined by special Deputy Ed St. Clair of Flagstaff and Carl Holton, a detective for the Santa Fe. The posse left for Canyon Diablo on the morning of March 22, 1889. By then — two days after the robbery — a $4,000 reward had been posted.

They picked up the outlaws' trail and followed it north to Lees Ferry. During the chase the posse dispatched a Navajo courier to alert communities in Utah to be on the lookout for the fugitives. (By the late 1880s, sheriffs were appointed U.S. deputy marshals, allowing them to cross county, state, or territorial lines in pursuit of outlaws.)

Word of the four fugitives had reached residents of the little Mormon community of Cannonville, Utah, located in the valley just east of Bryce Canyon. Not long after, the four men rode into town. The Mormons treated them with reserved kindness, fed them, and offered them a place to sleep. The four hard-looking strangers cautiously accepted the hospitality and settled in for the night. While the trail-weary train robbers were sleeping, the local constable, along with a posse of farmers, got the drop on them — briefly. Somehow, J.J. Smith was able to turn the tables. He nabbed the constable, who then told his band to throw down their guns. The outlaws then took supplies, fired a few indignant shots in the air, and — changing directions to confuse the posse — turned back towards Wahweap Canyon and Lees Ferry.

Buckey O'Neill and his posse rode into Cannonville a short time after the outlaws had fled. The posse put spurs to their horses and rode hard into the night. At Wahweap Canyon the posse found fresh tracks and warm campfire ashes. Nearby was a steer carcass. They followed the tracks up the canyon and spotted Smith, acting as lookout.

Unwittingly, the outlaws had boxed themselves in. Surrounded on three sides by steep cliffs, they spurred their mounts and charged toward the lawmen.

O'Neill jacked the lever on his Winchester and brought down Smith's horse. With that, bullets began buzzing around like hornets. One shot hit O'Neill's horse between the eyes. The animal went down pinning the sheriff to the ground for a few nervous moments. The furious gunfire frightened the outlaws' horses, causing them to stampede

**THE CANYON DIABLO POSSE:
(FROM LEFT) CARL HOLTON, JIM BLACK,
BUCKEY O'NEILL, AND ED ST. CLAIR**

into the brush. Now, the gang was afoot.

Halford and Sterin were captured, but Smith and Harvick made a run for it. They leaped over a bluff and bounced down to the canyon floor. The two were able to dodge the lawmen the rest of that day and through the night, crawling through brush and over rocky crevasses. Finally, they arrived at a small watering hole, footsore, thirsty, and tired.

They bathed their swollen feet in the cool water and were about to leave when a shot crashed into a rock, peppering them with pieces of granite. Weary and dispirited, the outlaws surrendered. By this time the lawmen had been in the saddle for three weeks and 600 miles.

The outlaws were taken to a Mormon community where the local blacksmith shackled them. Rather than take the long horse ride back to Arizona, O'Neill opted to take the captives by train to Salt Lake City, Denver, Trinidad, Albuquerque, and Arizona. Since news of the daring chase and gunfight was spread by the media, crowds gathered at every stop along the way to catch a glimpse of the notorious train robbers and to talk to Buckey O'Neill.

On the night the train reached Raton Pass near the Colorado-New Mexico border, J.J. Smith managed to slip out of his shackles and escape through a train window. He stole a horse and was heading to Texas when he ran into a raging blizzard. During the storm he chanced upon a young woman nearly dead from exposure.

Smith realized that if he stopped to help the woman she would be able to identify him to pursuing lawmen. There must have been some good in that cowboy-turned-outlaw, for he gallantly gathered in the woman and took her to safety. He was captured later in the Texas Panhandle town of Vernon and was returned to Arizona to stand trial.

Meanwhile, the other three outlaws were taken to Prescott without further incident. They were indicted on train robbery charges and faced the death penalty because on the day of the robbery the territorial Legislature had passed a law making train robbery, accompanied by display or discharge of firearms, a crime punishable by hanging.

Fearing the death penalty, the three outlaws pleaded guilty in exchange for prison sentences. On June 5, 1889, each of the three marauders was sentenced to 25 years at the Yuma Territorial Prison. But the boys got out after just a few years behind bars. Dan Harvick was released on Christmas Day, 1896. John Halford and Bill Sterin were freed nearly a year later, on November 1, 1897.

The noble J.J. Smith was brought to trial in November, 1889. He pleaded guilty and received a 30-year sentence — the extra five years was added for his escape.

Nonetheless, he was freed before the others. He was pardoned and released from prison on August 13, 1893, on condition that he leave Arizona and not come back. The fact that he forfeited his chances for escape by saving a life made a favorable impression on the territorial governor. After all, there really was a Code of the West.

There is more to this story. The young woman may have helped get Smith released early from prison.

Will Barnes stated how, "… her efforts were successful in securing his pardon (and make) a romantic story in itself." According to that version, the woman, a school teacher, was so remorseful over being responsible for Smith's capture she took her life savings, moved to Phoenix, and spent the next four years trying to persuade the governor to release him. The story goes on to say the governor finally agreed to a pardon. By this time, Smith and the lady were in love, got married and lived happily ever after. Nice story.

J.J. Smith himself told a different story. He claimed the only thing he ever heard about the damsel in distress was a story in a newspaper that told about how she had claimed a piece of the reward for his re-capture.

As for Bill Sterin, he enlisted in the First United States Volunteer Cavalry — the Rough Riders — when war broke out with Spain in 1898. So did Buckey O'Neill. Both were killed in the Battle of San Juan Hill.

Commodore Perry Owens: He Shoots It Out With Four Gunmen

Named after a naval hero, this gunfighter patrolled vast Apache County. He earned a reputation of being quiet, honorable, popular, and courageous. Among his adversaries were members of the Clanton gang, who had departed Tombstone after their battle with the Earps.

———❖———

W HEN OLD-TIME SHOOTERS SITTING AROUND GUNFIGHTers' Valhalla reminisce about the great shooting sheriffs in the Old West, Apache County Sheriff Commodore Perry Owens is certain to be mentioned. Owens did not gain the attention that many Wild West figures did. But his shoot-out with four gunmen ranks among the Old West's most sensational events.

In those days Apache County was a vast, rugged area of some 20,940 square miles, larger than Vermont and New Hampshire combined. Originally a part of Yavapai County, Apache County was created in 1879. The cattle ranges were overrun with rustlers. One report claimed 52,000 cows were rustled in one year alone, yet convictions for outlawry were rare.

The situation had become so desperate that in the fall of 1887 the Apache County Stock Association hired a range detective to eliminate a few of the most rapacious outlaws in hopes of putting the others to flight. Only two men in the organization knew the identity of the regulator and they were sworn to secrecy. The association used its entire savings, some $3,000, for bounty money, and used its political influence to have the hired gun appointed a United States deputy marshal.

Acting as judge, jury, and executioner, the gunman moved swiftly. He shot down two well-known rustlers who "resisted arrest." He then read warrants over their bodies. The six-gun justice served up by a mysterious avenging angel struck terror in the hearts of outlaws and sent many of them scurrying for other pastures.

There were some who later claimed that Commodore Perry Owens also was brought in by the association as a hired gun. True or not, he did much to cut down on the population of cow thieves in Apache County.

Commodore Perry Owens was born in Tennessee on July 29, 1852, the anniversary of Commodore Oliver Hazard Perry's great naval victory against the British on Lake Erie in the war of 1812. Owens' early years are obscure. Some say he left an abusive family and drifted to Texas in the early 1870s and became a cowboy. Later he headed for Oklahoma, where he took a job breaking horses.

As a young man he hunted buffalo on the plains, probably to supply railroad crews building westward. He stood 5 feet 10 inches, had light blue eyes, and a slight, sinewy frame. His most distinguishing feature was his shoulder-length hair, worn in the style of the mountain men and buffalo hunters. He was a simple, charismatic man of few words, and when he did speak it was with a drawl.

A famous photograph of Owens, the long-haired sheriff wearing his pistol butt forward and holding an antique Springfield rifle, likely was posed with studio props.

Owens was a typical gunfighter, the Old West's rendition of the Knights of the Round Table. He had a love of adventure and moved freely around Texas, Kansas, Oklahoma, Colorado, New Mexico, and Arizona. He was a man of action and extremely cool under pressure, as he would demonstrate one September day in Holbrook.

He arrived in Apache County in 1881 and worked for several cow outfits. For a time he guarded horses for a stagecoach company at Navajo Springs, near the New Mexico border. He had several brushes with local Navajos over disputed stock, and it was said they came to view him as an invisible ghost because their bullets never seemed to hit, while his "magic" guns never missed. Owens' experience as a buffalo hunter had turned him into an expert marksman, a skill that would come in handy that fateful day in Holbrook.

Owens had a reputation for courage and integrity. One newspaper was quoted as saying: "Mr. Owens is a quiet, unassuming man, strictly honorable and upright in his dealings with all men, and is immensely popular." He took few men into his confidence and had few intimate friends. According to old-timers, he cut a romantic swath with the pretty ladies around Concho and St. Johns.

By 1886, Owens was working as a deputy sheriff in Apache County. On November 4, he was elected sheriff, handily defeating incumbent John Lorenzo Hubbell of trading post fame.

COMMODORE PERRY OWENS

Social strife afflicted that part of the country at the time: Mormons against Mexicans around St. Johns; New Mexico sheepmen and Arizona cattlemen fighting over the grazing ranges; and the Hashknife outfit trying to rid the country of nesters.

Newspapers rejoiced at Owens' election, proclaiming he would end lawlessness in the county. Individuals celebrated, too. In Holbrook celebrants were firing their pistols in the air. George Lee got so caught up in the excitement, he accidentally shot his finger off.

Owens received strong support from the Mormons, and it was likely their votes that ensured his election. The previous administration had been anti-Mormon and had slandered them on matters concerning religious beliefs. Also, the Mormons believed Owens was the man to bring law and order to that part of the territory. Up to that time Owens hadn't done anything to cause so much public adulation. He was a man of honesty and integrity — that was certainly a refreshing change in politics, and he was known as a dead shot with rifle and pistol.

Owens' honesty was quickly demonstrated in the way he handled the expenses of the sheriff's office, right down to costs incurred for postage stamps. He cleaned up the county jail, which he described in a report as in a "horribly, filthy condition."

As to rustling, he went after the Clanton gang. Ike and Phin Clanton had moved their rustling operations to the Springerville area after their ill-fated run-in with the Earps and Doc Holliday in Cochise County in the early 1880s. One of Owens' deputies, "Rawhide" Jake Brighton, caught up with them on June 1, 1887, at the headwaters of Eagle Creek. Ike was killed and Phin was captured, tried, and given a 10-year sentence in the territorial prison at Yuma. A brother-in-law, Erbin Stanley, was told to get out of Arizona within 60 days.

Sheriff Commodore Perry Owens didn't always find success in his pursuit of outlaws. An example was Red McNeil, a reckless, carefree Hashknife cowboy who, at the age of 20, decided to become a desperado. He might not be remembered in the annals of outlawry if he hadn't had a propensity for leaving clever poems at the scene of his crimes. Usually they were meant to insult the lawmen chasing him. Red was believed to have come from an affluent family back East and had gone to college. He once confided to a friend that he had been educated to become a Catholic priest.

In early 1888, Red was in jail in Phoenix on a charge of horse stealing but escaped and stole another horse. He was recaptured and locked up in Florence but got away again. This time Red headed for Apache County, where he took a load of buckshot while attempting to rob Schuster's merchandise store in Holbrook. Red was making his getaway but still found time to pen this poem and tack it to a tree on the banks of the Little Colorado River:

I'm the prince of the Aztecs;
I am perfection at robbing a store;
I have a stake left me by Wells Fargo,
And before long I will have more.

There are my friends, the Schusters,
For whom I carry so much lead;
In the future, to kill this young rooster,
They will have to shoot at his head.
Commodore Owens says he wants to kill me;
To me that sounds like fun.
'Tis strange he'd thus try to kill me,

The red-headed son-of-a-gun.

He handles a six-shooter neat,
And hits a rabbit every pop;
But should he and I happen to meet,
We'll have an old-fashioned Arkansas hop.

Not much chance for a Pulitzer Prize, but not bad for an outlaw on the run.

Red McNeil crossed the border and hired out at the WS Ranch in New Mexico. The affable redhead entertained the cowhands with his mouth harp and clog dancing. Everyone thought he was a great guy until he vanished, taking with him the ranch's prize thoroughbred stud.

Near the Arizona-New Mexico border, Sheriff Owens rode into a cow camp one night asking if anyone was acquainted with the redheaded outlaw. None of the cowhands owned up to knowing him. The lawman was invited to stay the night. But he had no bedroll, so one of the punchers generously offered to share his blankets.

The cowhands rode out at daybreak, leaving Owens asleep. He awoke to find a note in familiar handwriting from the man who shared his bedroll:

Pardon me, sheriff
I'm in a hurry;
You'll never catch me
But don't you worry. — Red McNeil

Sheriff Owens' reaction to this affront is not known.

In 1889, the law finally caught up with the devil-may-care outlaw. He was arrested and convicted on a charge of train robbery and served 10 years in prison. In prison he taught himself to be a hydraulic engineer and went on to live a respectable life. Many years later he returned to Holbrook and visited Schuster's store. The former outlaw repentantly hoped there were no hard feelings, and he was assured the past was all water under the bridge.

Before the railroad arrived in 1881, Holbrook, located at the confluence of the Rio Puerco and Little Colorado, was known as Horsehead Crossing. The community was renamed Holbrook in 1882 for H.R. Holbrook, who was the first engineer on the Santa Fe (Atlantic and Pacific) Railroad. By 1887, the town had about 250 residents. Businesses included a Chinese restaurant run by a man named Louey Ghuey, Nathan Barth's store, Schuster's store, and five or six saloons including the notorious Bucket of Blood. The "socially elite" included the gamut of colorful frontier types: *filles de joie*, gamblers, sheepherders, cowboys, and railroaders.

There were a dozen or so frame shacks lined up along Main Street, which paralleled the Santa Fe railroad tracks. The Little Colorado River, or *Rio Chiquito Colorado*, ran just south of Main Street. North of the tracks, a blacksmith shop, livery stable, and several small houses lined Center Street. One of the houses recently had been occupied by members of the Blevins family.

(The town had no church and would not until 1913. During that period Holbrook had the distinction of being the only county seat in the United States without a church. And one came only after Mrs. Sidney Sapp cajoled her lawyer husband into organizing a fund to build one.)

For Sheriff Commodore Perry Owens, events were

moving rapidly towards his rendezvous with destiny. For a gunfighter to get into Valhalla he must have a strong antagonist. That antagonist would appear in the form of a vicious killer named Andy Cooper Blevins.

Andy Cooper Blevins arrived in Arizona from Texas around 1884. Some old accounts refer to him as "Cooper Blevins." Actually, his name was Andy Blevins, but he used Cooper as an alias. He was the oldest son of Martin Blevins, patriarch of the ill-fated Blevins family. Only 23 years old, Andy Blevins had been in trouble with the law since his youth.

Andy Blevins was born on the family ranch near Austin, Texas. He was run out of Indian Territory for peddling whiskey to Indians, and Texas lawmen wanted him on murder and robbery charges. One story had him escaping from the Texas Rangers by jumping from a train.

According to L.J. Horton's memoirs, Andy Blevins robbed and murdered a sheepherder in cold blood near Flagstaff. Blevins netted $30 for the crime. He then ambushed and killed a witness named Converse and the two lawmen who were pursuing him.

Blevins was considered a good man with a gun and was also a vicious bully. He especially enjoyed throwing his weight around peaceful Mormons in Arizona's Rim Country. According to one story, he ordered a family off its land along Canyon Creek at gun point because he wanted the place to rebrand stolen livestock. Other examples of his hooliganism were pistol-whipping an unarmed sheepherder, stealing Navajo horses, and browbeating local settlers. In short, Andy Cooper Blevins didn't seem to possess any redeeming qualities.

He encouraged his father, Martin Blevins, to bring the family to Arizona from Texas around 1886. Martin Blevins had five wild sons. Besides Andy, there were Charley, Hampton, John, and Sam.

Andy wasn't the only one to run afoul of the law. Hamp, the third-born, had done time in the Texas state prison for horse stealing. Martin, himself, had a fondness for good horseflesh and probably thought the change of scenery would do him and his family good.

He couldn't have been more wrong.

Andy Blevins, along with other members of his family, stole horses in Utah, Colorado, and northern Arizona and drove them to a lair at Canyon Creek, about 75 miles south of Holbrook. In early 1887, a long-simmering feud between the Tewksburys and Grahams in Pleasant Valley was heating up, and the Blevins boys joined the Graham faction.

In June, 1887, Martin Blevins left the ranch on Canyon Creek to look for horses. When he didn't return, Hamp and some friends went searching. They met three ex-Hashknife cowboys, John Paine, Tom Tucker, and Bob Gillespie, who were looking for some action.

They decided to ride into Pleasant Valley searching for the "Old Man," and, as one of them said, "start a little war of our own." They stopped off at the Graham ranch and added a few more gunmen to their little army.

On August 9, they rode brazenly up to the Middleton ranch and invited themselves to dinner. What ensued was a heated exchange with members of the Tewksbury faction, which included Jim Roberts, who would emerge as top gun in the feud. A fusillade of gunfire roared through the camp and several cowboys toppled from their saddles.

Hamp Blevins and John Paine lay dead on the ground. Tucker and Gillespie both suffered serious wounds. The Tewksburys suffered no casualties. The "little war" in Pleasant Valley had begun.

A few days later, 18-year-old Billy Graham was shot and killed by Tewksbury partisan Jim Houck, who was also a deputy for Sheriff Owens. The two met on a lonely trail and, after exchanging wary looks, went for their six-guns. Houck was the better man that day.

Thirsting for revenge, Andy Blevins and some Graham partisans decided to even things up with a sneak attack on the Tewksbury ranch. On the morning of September 2, 1887, they concealed their horses and quietly surrounded the ranch house. Inside were Ed Tewksbury, Sr. and his wife, Lydia; sons Ed and Jim; a daughter-in-law, Mary Ann; a schoolteacher, Mrs. Crouch; Jim Roberts; and some children.

Another son, John, and Bill Jacobs were outside gathering horses, unaware that several Winchesters were trained on them. The two men were walking back toward the cabin and passed a large boulder when rifle shots smashed the stillness of the morning. Jacobs took three bullets in the back. He staggered forward a few feet then fell to the ground face down. John Tewksbury took a bullet in the neck and went down writhing in pain. One of the assassins, quite possibly Andy Blevins, walked up and pumped three more slugs into him, then picked up a large boulder and crushed his skull.

The Graham partisans then turned their attention to the ranch house, peppering the building with gunfire. Inside, the Tewksburys and Roberts fought a desperate battle against the larger force outside. Then, to the horror of those inside the cabin, a drove of range hogs began to devour the bodies of Tewksbury and Jacobs. Calls for a truce to remove the bodies were refused by Tom Graham.

Andy Blevins wanted to scalp John Tewksbury but Graham forbade it. Blevins also wanted to set fire to the cabin and burn the Tewksburys out, but because of the women and children inside, Graham also vetoed that plan.

The Grahams placed snipers outside the cabin. For the next three days they fired on anyone who dared set foot outside. However, Mary Ann Tewksbury, who was expecting a baby, crept out at night and covered the bodies of her husband and Jacobs with bed clothing held down with rocks to keep the hogs from further devouring the bodies.

Jim Roberts was able to slip away and rode to Payson for help. A posse sent to the ranch drove the Graham partisans away. A coroner's jury and burial party finally arrived 11 days after the killings.

Andy Blevins must have left Pleasant Valley soon after the killing of Tewksbury and Jacobs. That Sunday morning, two days later, he was in Holbrook boasting that he had "killed one of the Tewksburys and another man whom he didn't know, on Friday ..."

Will C. Barnes, writing in *Apaches and Longhorns,* mentions that Sheriff Owens had held a warrant for Andy Blevins' arrest for some time but had been reluctant to serve it. Barnes claimed Owens and Blevins were old friends and Owens knew if he tried to arrest the desperado there would be a gunfight and one or both would be killed.

Also, there were reports that impatient county officials had ordered Owens to make the arrest of Andy Blevins or turn in his badge.

In September, 1887, just a few days after the gunfight at the Tewksbury Ranch, Barnes was working cattle about 10 miles from Holbrook when he got word of the pending showdown between the sheriff and Andy Blevins. He high-tailed it into town to witness the action.

"I wanted to see how the little affair would come off," he wrote in his book.

A short time after Blevins arrived in Holbrook, Owens rode into town from the south on a blaze-faced sorrel. He was met by Deputy Sheriff Frank Wattron at Sam Brown's stable. John Blevins, one of Andy's brothers, was at the stable when the sheriff arrived, but slipped away to warn his brother.

Justice D.G. Harvey was also present. He later testified that Owens, upon arriving, asked if Blevins was in town. When told he was, Owens said, "I am going to take him in." The sheriff then calmly proceeded to clean and reload his pistol.

Sam Brown offered to go along with Owens to help make the arrest of Andy Blevins, but Owens told him: "If they get me, it's all right. But I want you and everyone else to stay out of it."

Owens then cradled his Winchester in his arm and started for the Blevins house, about a hundred yards away. As he approached the house he saw a man watching him from an open door. As he drew closer, the door slammed shut. It was now about four o'clock in the afternoon.

After John Blevins left the stable he found his brother at the family home. Andy told John to get his horse from the stable and bring it to the house. John did as he was told, tying the dun-colored horse to a wagon outside the house.

Andy Blevins was throwing a saddle on the animal

when he looked up and saw Owens approaching. He quickly turned and went into the house.

Inside were two other men — John Blevins and Mote Roberts — and 15-year-old Sam Houston Blevins. Also present were Sam's mother, Mary Blevins, and her nine-year-old Artimesia; John's wife, Eva, and their infant son; and Amanda Gladden, her baby, and her nine-year-old daughter.

Frank Wattron, like many others, wanted a front row seat. He hustled to the railroad station and sat down next to Will Barnes. What happened next is perhaps best described by Commodore Perry Owens:

> I came in town on the fourth instant, went to Mr. Brown's Stable, put up my horse and about that time Mr. Harvey and Mr. Brown came into the stable. I spoke something of Mr. Cooper, and they told me he was in town, that he come in this morning. I told Mr. Brown that I wanted to clean my six shooter, that I was going to arrest Cooper if he was in town. I came in to clean my six-shooter. Someone came after a horse in the corral (John Blevins).

> Mr. Brown says to me, "That fellow is going to leave town."

> I told Mr. Brown to go saddle my horse, if he got away I would follow him. I did not wait to clean my pistol. I put it together without cleaning it, went into the stable, asked the man who cleans the horses if that man had saddled that dun horse. He said no.

> I says "Where is his saddle?"

> He says, "His saddle is down to the house."

I asked him where the house was. He told me the first one this side of the blacksmith shop. I went and got my Winchester and went down to arrest Cooper (Andy Blevins). Before I got there, I saw someone looking out at the door. When I got close to the house, they shut the door. I stepped up on the porch, looked through the window and also looked in the room to my left. I see Cooper and his brother (John) and others in that room. I called to Cooper to come out. Cooper took out his pistol and also his brother took out his pistol. Then Cooper went from that room into the East room. His brother came to the door on my left, took the door knob in his hand and held the door open a little. Cooper came to the Door facing me from the East room. Cooper held this door partly open with his head out.

I says, "Cooper, I want you."

Cooper says, "What do you want with me?"

I says, "I have a warrant for you."

Cooper says, "What warrant?"

I told him the same warrant that I spoke to him about some time ago that I left in Taylor, for horse stealing.

Cooper says, "Wait."

I says, "Cooper, no wait."

Cooper says, "I won't go."

I shot him.

This brother of his to my left behind me jerked open the door and shot at me, missing me and shot the horse which was standing side and a little behind me. I whirled my gun and shot at him, and then ran out in the street where I could see all parts of the house. I could see Cooper through the window on his elbow with his head towards the window. He disappeared to the right of the window. I fired through the house expecting to hit him between the shoulder. I stopped a few moments. Some man (Mose Roberts) jumped out of the house on the northeast corner out of a door or window, I can't say, with a six shooter in his right hand and his hat off. There was a wagon or buckboard between he and I.

I jumped to one side of the wagon and fired at him. Did not see him any more. I stood there a few moments when there was a boy (Sam Houston Blevins) jumped out of the front of the house with a six shooter in his hands. I shot him. I stayed a few moments longer. I see no other man so I left the house. When passing by the house I see no one but somebody's feet and legs sticking out the door. I then left and came on up town."

Owens' testimony was later substantiated by many other witnesses.

In the span of 60 furious seconds Owens had faced four gunmen. Only one, John Blevins, had gotten a shot off, and it missed. Owens fired four times. He didn't miss. Sam Blevins died instantly of a bullet in the chest. Mote Roberts lingered a few days before expiring, and John Blevins eventually recovered from a shoulder wound. Andy Cooper lived a few hours, suffering painfully from his wounds before giving up the ghost, and perhaps had some time to reflect on his savage life.

At the inquest, the Blevins family claimed Andy was

unarmed, which seems odd considering he was a notorious desperado and knew the sheriff was coming.

Witness D.B. Holcomb testified about the shooting of Sam Blevins, "If the boy had a pistol I did not see it."

Amanda Gladden claimed she never saw any of the Blevins men holding weapons.

Mary Blevins, Sam's mother, said, when asked if her son had a pistol, "Not that I know of. If he did I don't remember it."

But Dr. T.P. Robinson, who attended the youngster, testified he was holding a pistol. And the testimony of several other reliable witnesses, including Frank Wattron, Henry F. Banta, and Will Barnes, supported the sheriff.

In the end, an inquest exonerated Owens in the killing of all three men. A few days later, the *St. Johns Herald* said, "Too much credit cannot be given Sheriff Owens in this lamentable affair. It required more than ordinary courage for a man to go single-handed and alone to a house where it was known there were four or five desperate men inside, and demand the surrender of one of them. … Outside of a few men, Owens is supported by every man, woman and child in town."

Mary Blevins was the real casualty. Matriarch of the family, she had lost her husband, Martin, and son, Hamp, a few weeks earlier in the Pleasant Valley feud. Two more sons died in the fight with Owens, and another was seriously wounded. A month later another son, Charlie, would be gunned down by a posse while resisting arrest outside the Perkins Store in Pleasant Valley. His death was related to the Pleasant Valley feud. (The war in Pleasant Valley was considered long over when Ed Tewksbury shot and killed Tom Graham on a road outside Tempe on August 2,

1892. By then, Graham had left Pleasant Valley, married, and settled in the Tempe area on a farm. It was estimated that some 30 men died during the feud.)

John Blevins, who was wounded in the Holbrook shoot-out, was sentenced to five years in the Yuma Territorial Prison for his part but was released without serving any time. He later became a deputy sheriff and, in 1901, was shot in the shoulder by drunken soldiers just a few feet from the old Blevins house. He eventually moved to Phoenix, where he engaged in ranching. In 1928, he was appointed Arizona state cattle inspector. Two years later he was killed by a hit-and-run driver near Buckeye.

Civic leaders in Apache County became antagonistic towards Owens after the gunfight. One time, after the board of supervisors refused to pay Owens money he was owed, he walked into a meeting, drew his revolver, and demanded to be paid. The supervisors quickly paid up.

After his term expired Owens drifted around northern Arizona. He was a special agent for the Santa Fe Railroad for a time then an express messenger for Wells Fargo. Later he served as a U.S. Deputy Marshal for several years. In 1902, he settled in Seligman and married Elizabeth Barrett.

He had hung up his shooting irons by this time and ran a successful mercantile business until he died on May 10, 1919.

CHAPTER EIGHT

George Ruffner:
Sheriff Of Old Yavapai

*He enjoyed the pleasures of Prescott's
Whiskey Row, but he was much more than
a reveler. George Ruffner was elected sheriff
more than any other lawman in Arizona.
After a long chase, he hanged the cowboy
who had taught him cowboy skills.*

⇒◆⇐

THE LATE BUDGE RUFFNER USED TO TELL A STORY ABOUT his Uncle George's disdain for the political arena. George was sheriff of Yavapai County, and a good one. But he hated campaigning for office. Other politicians made long-winded political speeches. George simply walked to the podium and said, "I'm George Ruffner, I'm running for sheriff." Then he would sit down.

There was a man in town named Sandy Huntington. Sandy was from the prominent Huntington family in California but he had a serious drinking problem and was something of an embarrassment at family gatherings, so he was banished to Arizona. The sheriff took sympathy on Sandy and gave him odd jobs to do around the Ruffner livery stable. In return, Sandy gave Ruffner loyalty.

One election year George Ruffner was getting some stiff competition, and Sandy became concerned because the sheriff refused to campaign vigorously. By election day, the race was too close to call. Sandy volunteered to work at the voting booth assisting illiterate voters. The law required that the inability to read and write should not keep people from voting. Sandy's job was to read names of the candidates to illiterates and mark their ballots.

In relating the names of candidates for sheriff, he would say, "Democrat, George Ruffner; Republican, Pinky Graveldinger."

If the voter said, "Sandy, I want to vote for George Ruffner," Sandy would reply happily, "One vote for Sheriff Ruffner." And he would mark an X in the square next to George Ruffner's name.

However, if the voter wanted to vote for "that Republican fella," Sandy would mark an X in the square next to George Ruffner anyway and say with assurance, "By God, we'll just cross out that Democrat SOB!"

It's hard to say how much Sandy Huntington helped George Ruffner win elections but one thing is certain: Ruffner was elected to office more times than any other sheriff in Arizona history.

His family roots were already planted in Arizona history when George was born around 1862. His uncle, Morris. A. "Andy" Ruffner, was one of the first Americans to mine copper at Cleopatra Hill, high above the Verde Valley, where the town of Jerome would be established.

Tall and lanky, at 6 feet 4 inches, George rose above the crowd. He was a popular sheriff with a reputation for fair play. An intrepid, fearless lawman, he always got his man. It was said he could track bees in a blizzard.

George also liked to take in the games of chance in the gambling joints along Whiskey Row in Prescott. It was said he lost $1,700 one night on the turn of a single card.

SHERIFF GEORGE RUFFNER

It also was said he lost $38,000 on the night before gambling was outlawed in 1907.

Fortune did smile on him occasionally.

One night in a game of six-card stud in the Palace Saloon he won the Prescott mortuary that still bears his name. He won with a pair of sixes, and sometime later he bought a ranch outside of Prescott and registered his brand, two sixes or 66.

On July 14, 1900, a typical Saturday evening, Ruffner looked at the drunks celebrating on Whiskey Row and mused: "We'd have to wall-in the whole town and put a roof over it if we had to lock up all the drunks tonight."

That evening some miner came in from his shift, jammed his candle holder in the wall, with the candle still burning, and hurried off to the saloons. A fire started and quickly spread through the wooden frame buildings in the business district. Volunteer firefighters from clubs with colorful names like Dudes and Toughs fought valiantly through the night.

As the fire spread towards the Palace Saloon, customers picked up the priceless back bar, along with its contents, and carried them across the street to safety. They also saved the piano. That night, as Prescott burned, the bartender continued to serve drinks, and the piano player played. The most requested song: *There'll Be A Hot Time In The Old Town Tonight.*

Ruffner saved most of the town when he led a party of powder men into an area ahead of the fire. They dynamited the structures, halting the fire's spread.

They tell a story in Yavapai County of a time when Ruffner was on the trail of some dangerous outlaw. He knew the man was a crack shot with a Winchester. So Ruffner took off his hat and tied a neckerchief around his head. Then he tied up his stirrups and covered his saddle with a tarp to make it look like a pack. His deception complete, Ruffner ambled towards the outlaw's camp pretending to be a lonely old sheepherder leading a pack horse.

The scheme worked, and the unsuspecting bandit allowed Ruffner to walk into camp. Ruffner had the drop and made the arrest without incident.

Perhaps Ruffner's most sensational case was the pursuit and capture of Fleming (Jim) Parker.

Parker was a small-time cattle rustler and horse thief up around Peach Springs. Local ranchers considered him more of a nuisance than a real outlaw. He might never have been known outside his neighborhood if he hadn't decided to rob a Santa Fe train.

Parker was born in Visalia, California, in 1865. His mother died when he was young, and his father went insane when the boy was 14. A year later he was sentenced to a year and a half in San Quentin. Soon after being released from prison, Parker got crossways with the law again and headed for Arizona.

Parker hired on as a cowpuncher for the Thornton Ranch near the headwaters of the Agua Fria River in Yavapai County. He was only 17, but was rawhide tough and could cowboy with the best of them. He stood about 5 feet 8 inches, weighed about 160 pounds, and had brown, curly hair. He liked to wear his hat pushed back on his head.

Parker had been working for George Thornton about a year when 20-year-old George Ruffner hired on. Ruffner had been working for his uncle Andy as a miner. Parker taught him to ride and rope, the two most important skills for a cowboy. After about six months they drifted around Yavapai County, working at various cow ranches.

In 1881, after spring roundup at a ranch in Chino Valley, the boys drew their pay and headed for Prescott. Their arrival brought a turning point in their lives. George Ruffner would establish roots and call Prescott home for the rest of his life. Wild and woolly, Fleming Parker would continue to backslide towards his terrible end.

Prescott, the territorial capital, was bustling. The railroad wouldn't arrive until 1887, so supplies came to town by freight wagons from Colorado River ports at Hardyville and Ehrenberg. Other freight lines hauled through Yeager Canyon into Jerome and the Verde Valley. Also, there was freighting to an upstart community in the Salt River Valley called Phoenix, a hundred miles south.

George Ruffner decided to go into the freight business. Fleming Parker preferred the carefree life of a cowboy. As soon as his pay was spent, he would hire out again until he had enough money for another "whizzer" in town.

George married Molly Birchett, and through hard work and perseverance saw his business grow successfully. Pretty soon he added a livery stable and stage line to his business portfolio.

Parker, on the other hand, continued his reckless ways. He drifted back into California and got into trouble with the law. In 1890, he was sent up for six years at San Quentin. He was released early and by 1895 was back in Arizona. A year before Parker's return, George Ruffner was elected sheriff of Yavapai County

Parker hired out to "Hog-Eye" Miller at the Hat Ranch near Williams. Not long after Parker went to work for the Hat Ranch, cattle turned up missing. Then he took a job breaking horses for the local constable at Williams. Soon, some of them were missing.

Then he drifted over to Seligman, in Yavapai County. A short time after his arrival there, two rustlers were seen driving 40 head of horses from a holding pen. They drove them northwest up Aubrey Valley. Sheriff Ruffner and a posse rode the Bullock Line from Prescott to Seligman, then took out after the rustlers on horseback. They caught up with them near Fraziers Well. After a running gunfight, the lawmen recovered the horses but the two outlaws got away. Lawmen were sure one of them was Fleming Parker.

Parker's next haunt was Peach Springs, where he joined up with Abe Thompson, Windy Wilson, and Pug Marvin, a band of rascals known as the Thompson gang. Their activities included rustling livestock from ranches in that part of Arizona. The stolen animals usually were driven up Big Chino Valley north of Seligman, west to Robber's Roost Canyon, and to where Diamond Creek joins the Colorado River. The gang crossed the river and headed the animals into Nevada, where they sold them.

The gang also stole livestock in Nevada and brought them back to Arizona for sale. They generally preferred stealing horses to cows because they could be moved faster.

But train robbery offered a new dimension to the gang. Wells Fargo was known to ship thousands of dollars in gold by rail. Since the first transcontinental railroads had been built across northern and southern Arizona in the early 1880s, several heists had occurred in Arizona.

Parker studied all the operations of the trains and even learned the basics of running a locomotive. Then he laid out a plan to rob a train carrying gold from San Francisco through northern Arizona.

The heist was set to take place on February 8, 1897. Parker and one other gang member would rob the train as it passed through Rock Cut, between Peach Springs and Nelson. But first, Parker made a big show of going into town and catching a train for California after telling everyone he had a good job there. Then he caught another train at Barstow, California, and went into Nevada. He then rode back south to the gang's canyon hideout.

Meanwhile, the rest of the gang, except for Windy Wilson, rode into Peach Springs to establish an alibi.

Beginning the robbery, Parker and Wilson jumped on the train as it slowed on the grade at Rock Cut. Parker climbed into the cab, leveled his revolver at the engineer and ordered him to stop the train. Wilson rushed toward the express car. When the train stopped, Wells Fargo express car messenger Jim Summers became suspicious and stepped from the train with his pistol drawn. He spotted Wilson cutting the train in two by unhooking a linking latch. Wilson looked up and jerked his six-gun, but the Wells Fargo man had the drop. Two shots rang out and Wilson was dead.

Parker heard the two gunshots and thought they were a pre-arranged signal. So he ordered the engineer to take the train down the line. It wasn't until the train came to a halt where the robbers' horses were picketed that Parker realized that Wilson was missing and that the express car, which carried the gold, had been left behind. Wilson had separated the train in the wrong place, apparently because the express car was not in its usual position.

Parker rifled through pouches in the mail car, and in his haste, missed several thousand dollars in negotiable bonds. The disgusted outlaw then slipped away in the dark with a net gain of $5.

After the robbery Fleming Parker headed for his lair at Rustler's Roost Canyon. A posse led by George Ruffner was formed in Prescott.

Parker tried to confuse the lawmen by cutting back, criss-crossing, and circling around his pursuers. After nearly a week the posse got close enough to Parker to fire on him. But he was riding a rested animal, and the lawmen's horses were trail weary.

He escaped the hail of fire. Anticipating pursuit, Parker had cached food and supplies at strategic places in the rough country near the Colorado River.

The lawmen finally found Parker on February 22

north of Peach Springs, where Diamond Creek empties into the Colorado River. Two members of the posse, "One-Eye" Riley and Martin Buggeln, were gathering firewood when they stumbled upon Parker's camp. The outlaw was caught unawares and, looking down the barrels of two six-guns, surrendered without a fight.

Fleming Parker likely would have gotten a light jail sentence, for he had many friends in Yavapai County. But, on May 9, 1897, he, Lewis Miller, and Cornella Sarata broke from their cells. On the way out Parker grabbed a sawed-off shotgun. Deputy County Attorney Lee Norris overheard the commotion and came to investigate. He opened the door and ran into the three escapees. Norris started to retreat but was cut down with a load of buckshot. He died later that night.

The three fugitives headed for George Ruffner's livery stable. Parker, always the judge of good horseflesh, chose Sureshot, the sheriff's best horse and reputed to be the fastest horse in the territory. Ruffner had gotten the long-legged white horse from the Hashknife Ranch. The animal was part Arab and had great endurance.

Ruffner was in Congress when word of the jail break reached him. He commandeered a locomotive, rushed back to Prescott, and joined the posse at Point of Rocks.

The posse caught up with the escapees at Lynx Creek. Deputies opened fire and shot Miller's horse out from under him. Miller also took a bullet in the side and another in the leg. Parker pulled the wounded man up on the back of Sureshot and the two escaped in a hail of gunfire. During the flight Parker was shot in the leg.

The third escapee, Cornella Sarata, also was shot in

the leg at Lynx Creek. But he got away and never was captured. Some claimed he headed for Crown King, where he had relatives who smuggled him into Mexico. Others insisted he crawled off to some hidden place and died.

Parker and Miller decided to split up because Miller's wounds were giving him considerable pain. Parker kept riding southeast and Miller walked north for Jerome Junction in Chino Valley. At the junction, Miller followed the narrow-gauge railroad tracks east several miles to Jerome where a sister lived. For a couple of days he hid out in the appropriately named Deception Gulch. Finally he was able to make contact with her, and she persuaded him to surrender. Jerome Constable Jim Roberts, of Pleasant Valley War fame, and two other lawmen took Miller to the Coconino County jail at Flagstaff.

Meanwhile, Parker turned north, cleverly concealing his trail by crossing and re-crossing it. Using bloodhounds, the posse picked up his trail at Point of Rocks but quickly lost it again causing the local newspaper to quip, "the fox is smarter than the hounds."

Ruffner stubbornly kept up pursuit even though friends of Parker tried to thwart him. A note found pinned to a post offered a thousand-dollar reward for the sheriff, "dead or alive — dead preferred."

Cowboys who had known or ridden with Parker threatened to shoot the pursuers and their bloodhounds. The man who owned the bloodhounds wanted to quit the chase after someone stole his horses. Then Parker left a note offering to pay a ten-dollar reward for every bloodhound that was shot. That was the last straw. The owner took his beloved dogs and returned to Phoenix.

SURESHOT

Parker rode into a sheepherder's camp and swapped the shotgun for a Winchester. The wily fugitive also threw in a lost-treasure map in the deal. He told the herder he had buried $1,500 taken in the robbery in a can and said it was his for the taking. The grateful sheepherder then drove his flock over Parker's tracks and sent the posse on a wild goose chase.

When another herd of sheep wiped out a trail, Ruffner returned to Prescott to await further leads. The rumor mill began churning out sightings. It seemed the elusive Parker was everywhere and nowhere at the same time.

Still believing the posse was on his trail, Parker put

shoes backward on Sureshot and rode him some distance. Near Williams, he turned the white horse loose and stole another good horse from a rancher for whom he once worked. Then he rode into Williams and left his ex-boss's horse at a livery stable and stole another. This time he wrapped burlap around the animal's feet and rode west at a gallop.

Still, no one seemed to know the whereabouts of Fleming Parker. Lawmen believed many locals were sympathetic to the gregarious cowboy they knew when he worked for ranches in the area years before.

At the time lawmen were scouring the town, Parker was hiding out in a little cave in the mountains west of Williams. While at the cave, Parker was left afoot when his latest equine acquisition got loose and returned to the safe confines of the livery stable.

Lawmen got a break when someone spotted Parker walking near Hog-Eye Miller's Hat Ranch, a few miles west of Williams. Bloodhounds followed the scent right to the ranch house, but by this time Parker was gone.

His trail led up into the rough, lofty reaches of Bill Williams Mountain. They found a cave and warm coals showing the outlaw was close but the dogs got to sneezing and lost the trail. This time the foxy fugitive had spread pepper on his trail. Once again, Parker had outwitted his pursuers. The frustrated lawmen went home to await further developments. Meanwhile, Parker, riding a horse given him by Hog-Eye, was riding north into Navajo land.

The next break came on May 23 when two Navajos saw Parker's picture on a wanted poster at a trading post north of Tuba City. They had seen the fugitive crossing the Little Colorado River near Cameron. Navajos in the area kept Parker under surveillance while lawmen in

Flagstaff and Prescott were alerted. Soon, Sheriff Ruffner was hot on the trail again, this time in the arid desert north of the Little Colorado River. Thanks to the expert work of the Navajos keeping tabs on Parker's itinerary, lawmen from Coconino County were able to sneak up on his camp about sixty miles north of Tuba City and take him without a fight. He awoke to see several rifles pointed in his direction.

"Mornin', Parker," said Coconino Sheriff Ralph Cameron.

"Reckon it ain't so good for me," Parker mused.

Sheriff Ruffner arrived in time to meet the lawmen from Coconino County at a crossing on the Little Colorado. Parker is supposed to have said to Ruffner, "Where in hell would I have to go to find a place where you wouldn't be?"

And the trail-weary sheriff is supposed to have replied, "That's exactly where you'll be when I finish ridin' herd on you."

Parker later said he had planned to make another escape while they were fording the river by jerking a pistol from the holster of one of the Navajos and getting the drop on the others but gave up on the idea when Ruffner arrived.

Fleming Parker was then taken back to Flagstaff and placed in a cell next to his accomplice, Lewis Miller. Before leaving for Prescott by train, a blacksmith riveted leg irons on both prisoners.

The train passed through Williams without incident and pulled into Ash Fork later that evening where they changed trains and climbed aboard the Peavine for Prescott. Rumors of a lynch mob in Prescott had Ruffner uneasy. The train rolled quietly into Fort Whipple, just outside Prescott, late that night with its headlight off. A carriage was waiting to deliver the prisoners the rest of the way. It wouldn't have mattered as the expected crowd wasn't at the station, they were waiting at the courthouse. There were a few tense moments. Miller feared they were going to get lynched, but Parker chastised him saying, "have a little courage — they can only hang you once."

Ruffner wasn't in the mood for macho-talking townies. If the crowd had any plans for a necktie party, he quickly laid them to rest with some tough talk. The citizens were gruffly told to go home and the prisoners were returned to the scene of their escape three weeks earlier.

Parker went on trial June 15, 1897, before Judge John Hawkins for the murder of Lee Norris. The trial lasted three days and returned a guilty verdict. A few days later Judge Hawkins sentenced him to hang on August 13. Miller was given a life sentence at the Yuma Territorial Prison. He served only a few years and was released.

Appeals and delays postponed the execution until June 8, 1898.

The law required a certain number of witnesses and Sheriff Ruffner hadn't bothered to have invitations made for the hanging, so he dealt cards to witnesses from his personal deck. No one was allowed into the hanging grounds without a card.

On Parker's last night in jail before his hanging, Ruffner asked if he could bring him anything. Parker replied he would sure like to see Flossie, a *fille de joie* over on Whiskey Row, one more time. So the sheriff sneaked the obliging Flossie in through the back door of the jail and locked her in Parker's cell. Later that night he returned and escorted her back to the district.

On that final day, Parker, seeing daylight for the first time in a year, was led to the black-painted scaffold. He halted at the steps and asked if he could have a look around as he had never seen one before. His curiosity satisfied, he climbed the steps and surveyed the crowd. He saw an old friend and called, "Hello, Jack, how are they breaking?"

Parker announced on the scaffold that there was only one man he respected enough to pull the lever at his hanging and that was his old friend George Ruffner.

After his arms and legs were secured, Parker was asked if he had any last words. "I have not much to say," he offered, "I claim that I am getting something that ain't due me, but I guess every man who is about to be hanged says the same thing, so that don't cut no figure; whenever the people says I must go, I am the one who can go and make no kick."

As they started to place a black cover over his head, Parker asked to shake hands with the boys on the scaffold, then said to the jailer, " ... tell the boys I died game and like a man."

At 10:31 A.M. Sheriff Ruffner pulled the lever and his old friend-turned-adversary dropped six feet to eternity. At 4 o'clock that afternoon Fleming Parker was buried in a potter's plot. Hanging a man sickened Ruffner enough that he pressed to have future hangings take place at the territorial prison. Parker's was Prescott's last hanging.

There has been much lore surrounding the story of George Ruffner and Fleming (or Jim, as he was sometimes called) Parker. One story has it that Parker robbed the Santa Fe after one of its trains hit and killed one of his prize horses. When the railroad paid him a paltry sum, Parker robbed their train in revenge.

George Ruffner had a long and illustrious career as a lawman in Yavapai County and when he died in 1933, he was the state's oldest sheriff in age and seniority. Many years later he became the first Arizonan inducted into the National Cowboy Hall of Fame in Oklahoma City.

Sureshot spent his last years in Phoenix, on a small farm located at the site of the famous Biltmore Hotel. According to Budge Ruffner, he was the only member of the Ruffner family be buried at a five-star resort. After the chase in which Parker was riding Sureshot, some claimed that the deputies were firing high because none wanted to take a chance on shooting the sheriff's favorite horse.

The Good The Bad And The Ugly: The Saga Of Pancho Villa

*A saying in Mexico proclaimed that
Pancho Villa was hated by thousands, but
loved by millions. Besides in his own country,
the charismatic bandit-revolutionary left
his mark in border states such as Arizona,
where he was viewed as a bogeyman.*

———◆———

A BRIGHT ORANGE GLOW SPREAD ACROSS THE EASTERN New Mexico horizon on the morning of March 9, 1916. The border town of Columbus was mostly asleep. The first group of Mexican soldiers cut through the barbed wire and crossed quietly into the United States and began moving towards Columbus, three miles north.

About a mile from the slumbering town, General Francisco "Pancho" Villa divided his 500 raiders into two columns. One set out for the U.S. Army post at Camp Furlong, while the other went to strike Columbus.

Shouting "*mata los gringos!*" — death to the whites! — the raiders stormed the town, shooting civilians in cold blood as they ran out of their homes to see what all the commotion was about. Bullets were flying in all directions, breaking windows as the *pistoleros* rode up and down the streets. The wooden buildings of the business district were looted and set on fire. The invaders fired on any home with lights on.

At nearby Camp Furlong, the Mexicans encountered stiff resistance from the American troops, who quickly recovered from the surprise attack and opened fired with rifles and shotguns. The fire from the town lit the Mexicans, making them easy targets for the Americans.

One group of Villa's men ran into a kitchen, where angry cooks doused them with boiling water. At the stables, American soldiers attacked the raiders with pitchforks. Soon, the Americans opened fire with machine guns, forcing Villa's raiders to retreat to the border.

Nearly 140 of Villa's *bravos* were lost; 17 Americans were killed. It was the last attack on the continental United States by soldiers from a foreign nation.

Who was this enigma called Pancho Villa? Many people claimed he was Mexico's greatest military genius; others said he was second only to Santa Anna as Mexico's greatest scoundrel. Some compare him to Attila the Hun and Genghis Khan; others adore him as a national folk hero.

What drove Villa to attack the powerful United States, where he had many admirers who saw him as America's best friend among those who were fighting for power in the Mexican Revolution raging at the time?

The questions largely remain unanswered, but speculation has provided many theories: He was backing Germany; he wanted the vast stores of military weapons, especially the machine guns, kept at Camp Furlong; he wanted revenge against some American arms dealers who had reneged on a deal; he was trying to improve his stature among Mexicans who despised the United States; he was trying to involve the U.S. government in the Mexican revolution and show that his bitter political rival, Venustiano Carranza, was incapable of ruling Mexico. Some claimed Villa was hired to make the attack by American interests in Mexico who felt that a U.S. invasion of Mexico would protect their business interests.

Francisco "Pancho" Villa, was born in the settlement of Rio Grande in the Mexican state of Durango on June 5, 1878. It is said that on the night of his birth a severe thunderstorm occurred, and during the lightning, Venus, the evening star, changed its size and color. The humble Mexicans believed this celestial occurrence foretold a turbulent life for the baby named Doroteo Arango. His family was from a very low class, known in Mexico as *peones*.

As a child, Doroteo was different from the other children, causing people to say he was actually the son of an aristocrat who was a secret lover of his mother. This story only adds to the aura of mystery enveloping Pancho Villa.

The Arango family worked for a wealthy rancher named Lopez Negretes. When Doroteo was a youngster, his father became ill and died. Doroteo became head of the family, which included two sisters and two brothers.

Hoping to earn more money to support his family, Doroteo went to another ranch without Negretes' permission, but was brought home and beaten severely by the *patron*. After his wounds healed, Doroteo ran away again. He was caught again, and this time was thrown in jail, where he became friendly with some old bandits. They entertained him with colorful stories of life on the outlaw trail. Upon his release, the youngster had decided to become a *bandito.*

According to legend, Doroteo learned that while he was in jail his little sister, Mariana, was raped by Negretes' son, Leonardo. Doroteo returned to the ranch and shot Leonardo. He then rode off to the Sierra Madre mountains with a price on his head for murder. During the next few years he lived the life of a bandit, eventually becoming a *jefe,* or leader.

It likely was then that he took the name of a famous old outlaw he admired — Pancho Villa.

The Mexican Revolution of 1910 gave Pancho Villa the opportunity to get involved in a cause and make his countrymen forget that he was a bandit. He and his band joined the rebels in the first year of the fighting. At the age of 22, he was appointed a captain.

The dictator of Mexico at the time was Porfirio Diaz, who had ruled with an iron fist since the death of the legendary Benito Juarez in 1872.

Diaz's slogan was "Bread and the Club." Bread was for the elite, the army, the bureaucrats, the foreigners in Mexico, and even the Church. The club was for the common folks and those who chose to differ with him. Diaz enforced his slogan with the ruthless *Rurales* (rural guards), his personal police force.

Most of the revolutionaries fought to free Mexico from the dictator and create a democracy. At first, Villa was in the fight only for profit. Later, he became a believer in the revolutionary cause.

Pancho Villa idolized the revolution's leader, a California-educated visionary named Francisco Madero.

Unlike Villa, Madero was an aristocrat and a man of great learning. But they shared a love for Mexico.

In the months that followed Villa's joining the revolution, his forces won battles at Casas Grandes and Juarez. In May, 1911, Diaz resigned and went to France in exile. Madero became president.

But Madero was not able to appease all leaders of the revolution and fighting continued in Mexico. In 1912, Villa was jailed after he engaged in a dispute with General Victoriano Huerta, who had been sent to northern Mexico to quell an insurrection launched by a revolutionary. Villa escaped, and returned to the northern border.

In February, 1913, President Madero was forced to resign and he was killed on orders from Huerta, who had declared himself president. Huerta's presidency was punctuated with an orgy of drunkenness, robbery, and murder.

Villa, now a colonel in the army, hated Huerta and led his men to war against him. Villa's army grew with each victory. He recaptured Juarez and then Chihuahua City.

In capturing Juarez, Villa showed his military genius. Villa captured a *federale* troop train and wired the commander at Juarez. The message claimed the engine had broken down and requested another locomotive and five more box-cars. The commander in Juarez, believing he had heard from one of his own officers, complied. After the train arrived, Villa sent another telegram, saying the rebels were approaching from the south, cutting the telegraph lines. "What shall I do?"

The commander wired back: "Return at once!"

So, Villa's brigade boldly rode into Juarez on a

PANCHO VILLA DURING THE REVOLUTION

steam-driven Trojan horse in the middle of the night. By sunrise, Juarez was held by the *Villistas.*

Given command of the famous Division of the North, the former bandit now was one of the most powerful men in Mexico. Huerta soon was driven from power. In December, 1914, Villa's army rode triumphantly into Mexico City. This was the high point in Villa's life. He was now a hero throughout Mexico and was offered the presidency, but declined.

Another leader of the revolution was Emiliano Zapata, the great revolutionary hero of southern Mexico.

Witnesses said that while Zapata's troops begged for food in Mexico City, Villa's went on a drunken spree, raping and pillaging. Political rivals, such as Venustiano Carranza and Alvaro Obregon, conspired against Villa and Zapata. Eventually, Zapata would be treacherously murdered by those loyal to Carranza.

General Obregon's army attacked Villa's drunken, undisciplined troops and drove them back to Celeya, in the state of Guanajuato. There, in April, 1915, the bloodiest war in the revolution was fought. Villa's brave *Dorados* charged again and again against the barbed wire and machine gun emplacements of Obregon to no avail. In the end, Villa was soundly defeated and what was left of his army retreated back to his old haunts in northern Mexico. Villa was once again just a *bandito*.

Bloody battles raged between the armies of Villa and Carranza over the next several months. Many of these were near the American border towns of Del Rio in Texas and Naco, Douglas, and Nogales in Arizona. Curious Americans watched the battles from the roofs of buildings or from the tops of railroad boxcars located just north of the border.

During these turbulent years, this writer's father lived in Del Rio. My first history lessons came as a young-ster, listening to stories he told of watching the fighting between the two armies. Once he sat on the north bank of the Rio Grande for two days watching a battle between the *Carranzistas* and *Villistas.*

One time Villa got an American film company from Hollywood to make a war movie of one of his battles. He even offered to attack at a time of day when the light was best for the cameras.

A movie called *The Life of General Villa* was made but failed at the box office because the American audiences didn't think it was "realistic" enough.

Both sides hired American barnstorming pilots to fly over the other's trenches and drop homemade bombs. Probably, the first aerial combat in history took place in the skies over Naco, Sonora.

Dean Lamb and Phil Roder were a couple of American barnstorming pilots who joined the action. Lamb flew for Villa, while Roder was in the employ of the *federales.* The planes had no guns so the pair emptied their six-shooters at each other in the skies over Naco.

During a land battle near Douglas, several bullets flew into American homes. At one point the sheriff of Cochise County, Harry Wheeler, rode out between the armies carrying a white flag. He got the two opposing Mexican generals together and asked them to move their men so they wouldn't be shooting towards the American side. They obliged, and the battle resumed.

Although Pancho Villa had many friends in the United States, President Woodrow Wilson, in October, 1915, recognized Carranza's government and allowed him to move his troops on the American side of the border on American railroads. Wilson accused Villa of allowing his soldiers to murder, rape, and pillage the people of Mexico. It should be noted the *Carranzistas* were guilty of the same crimes. Villa was also accused of murdering many foreigners, including Americans.

By 1916, only the peasants still believed in Pancho Villa. He was convinced the Americans were the cause of his trouble and vowed to take revenge. Revenge came at Columbus, New Mexico.

After the raid on Columbus, Wilson ordered General John J. Pershing to take an armed force into Mexico to capture or kill Pancho Villa. Villa proved to be an elusive target. Rumors spread: Villa was supposed to be everywhere, attacking American cities from Texas to Arizona.

In Arizona he had become a ubiquitous Mexican bogeyman. One rumor had it that Villa and his men had ridden into Arizona with plans to blow up Theodore Roosevelt Dam, rob all the banks in the Salt River Valley, and wipe out the cities. Nervous bankers were issuing rifles to the citizenry, and women were taking Red Cross training to treat the expected wounded. Villa was, no doubt, amused by all the hysterical chaos he was creating.

The American Army chased Pancho Villa across the mountains and high deserts of Mexico for nearly a year. Apaches were used as scouts; troops drove across the sandy desert in primitive automobiles; and airplanes flew the skies. All searched in vain for the phantom *bandito.*

To the peasants, he became an even bigger hero. Legends about him grew. One story said that when the *Americanos* got close to Villa he transformed into an agave plant. Another claimed he became an antelope and outran his foes. Still another said he turned into a little black dog and was seen barking and nipping at the heels of his pursuers' horses.

Villa himself said the ghost of his dead mother came to him in a vision and warned him when the *Americanos* were getting close.

Eleven months after entering Mexico, the American Army returned to Texas. The so-called Punitive Expedition had failed in its mission to catch Villa. Still, the Americans had succeeded in scattering his army. In April, 1917,

America declared war on Germany and General Pershing was named commander of the American forces going to Europe. Mexico had proven to be a good training ground for the Americans. They could thank Pancho Villa for that.

The *Centauro del Norte* was quite a womanizer. The portly Villa wasn't handsome. He had adenoids and was a mouth breather, but his legendary status caused the ladies to vie for his attention.

He married at least seven times. Luz Corral was recognized by the government as his wife. During the 1970s she was asked by a reporter about the other wives, and she graciously replied: "They were his little churches. I was his cathedral!"

Villa had such a notorious reputation for taking women that he was credited — or blamed — with fathering many more children than he did. Many times when a woman became pregnant by someone other than her husband, she claimed Pancho was the father. No man could blame his wife for relenting to the amorous advances of such a forceful man; and certainly, no man was about to confront such a powerful man to defend her honor.

But Villa didn't always have his way with women. At Torreon his soldiers executed the aristocratic husband of a Spanish woman. He was quite taken by her beauty and asked her to dinner. She accepted, and while dining asked him to allow the Spaniards to remain in the city. He said he would if she would become his mistress. She refused, and he angrily exiled all Spaniards from the city.

Villa had a very dark, cruel side to his personality. He took pleasure forcing Mennonite fathers and husbands to watch as his men raped their wives and daughters.

Beneath that brutality was some compassion. A famous border song, *Adelita,* tells the story of one of Villa's sergeants, named Portillo. The sergeant and Adelita planned to be married, but she wanted one more fling. One night, she made a play for Villa, and Portillo saw them kissing. Broken-hearted, he shot himself. When Villa learned what had happened, he refused to see Adelita again. She joined his *Dorados* as a *soldaldera,* and soon was mortally wounded in battle. Villa had her buried in a handsome tomb in Parral, next to Portillo.

In 1919, Villa raised another army and vowed to defeat his enemy, Venustiano Carranza. In June, he conquered Juarez but allowed his troops to go on a drunken rampage, pillaging the town while firing shots at Americans across the border in El Paso. Actually, both *Villistas* and *Carranzistas* were shooting into El Paso.

The next morning, U.S. troopers from the black military units at Fort Bliss, Texas, stormed across the border. American artillery blasted a huge water tower above the race track where much of Villa's army was camped and literally washed the *Villistas* away. Pancho Villa's hung-over soldiers were routed. Villa escaped but his day in the sun was over.

He retired quietly to the mountains of the Sierra Madre, where he had begun. He found solace that Carranza and Obregon became political rivals and the former was driven from the presidency and murdered by one of his own officers in April, 1920. Obregon would ascend to the presidency and he, too, would die by the gun in 1928.

On Friday, July 20, 1923, Pancho Villa was driving home in his Dodge automobile near the town of Parral. He sat in the front seat with a woman and another friend. In the back seat were two bodyguards. As the auto passed a large tree, a pumpkin seed vendor raised his hand and shouted, "Viva Villa!" The general slowed and lifted a hand to salute the vendor.

At that moment gunfire opened up. The big auto spun in a cloud of dust. All the occupants except a bodyguard were killed. Pancho Villa was found slumped over the steering wheel with 16 bullets in his body.

There were seven gunman waiting for Villa that day. One, Jesus Salas Barragas, served six months in jail for the crime. He proudly claimed it wasn't murder — that he had rid the world of a monster.

Since those days, Pancho Villa has been analyzed, romanticized, lionized and criticized. If you ask, "Was Pancho Villa a good guy or bad?" I'll say he was the good, the bad, and the ugly rolled into one. Like others of his ilk, Villa was a product of his time and should be judged that way. He was no better or worse than some others in the turbulent years that rocked Mexico in the early part of the 20th century.

Arizona As Only *Arizon*

Tucson To Tombstone
In this guidebook, avid southeastern Arizona explorer Tom Dollar tells stories of the region and takes you over its trails. As you learn facts and legends of the Old West, you'll travel from desert floor to riparian canyons to alpine forests. Features maps, travel tips, and more than 128 full-color photographs. Softcover. 96 pages.
#ATTS6 $12.95

Arizona Ghost Towns and Mining Camps
Ghost town authority Philip Varney brings the Old West to life with captivating anecdotes and a gallery of rare, historic photographs. Regional maps, detailed travel information and a full-color photographic portfolio tell what each site is like today and make this fascinating history of Arizona's mining boom a reliable travel guide as well. Softcover. 136 pages. **#AZGS4 $14.95**

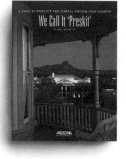

We Call It "Preskit"
Explore the frontier history and hometown charm of Prescott and the high country of central Arizona with author Jack August. The full-color book features things to see and do in the area, including Jerome. Softcover. 64 Pages. **#APRS6 $12.95**

Cow Pie Ain't No Dish You Take to the County Fair
That's just one of the cowboy witticisms in *Arizona Highways*' first humor book. Accompanied by Western cartoonist Jim Willoughby's whimsical illustrations, this collection of 165 jokes, riddles, and one-liners takes a fun and friendly look at the simple facts of cowboy life. You'll laugh out loud. Softcover. 144 pages. **#ACWP7 $6.95**

Ordering Information

To order these and other books and products write to:
Arizona Highways, 2039 West Lewis Avenue, Phoenix, AZ 85009-2893.
Or send a fax to 602-254-4505.
Or call toll-free nationwide 1-800-543-5432.
(In the Phoenix area or outside the U.S., call 602-258-1000.)
Visit us at http://www.arizhwys.com to order online.

ighways Can Present It

Manhunts & Massacres
Pieced together from the annals of Arizona's frontier days, here are 18 stories recounting cleverly staged ambushes, massacres that cried out for justice, and the valiant, sometimes vicious, pursuits staged by lawmen and Indian fighters. Softcover. 144 pages.
#AMMP7 **$7.95**

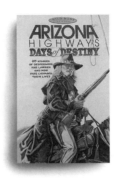

Days Of Destiny
This book features 20 historical stories about Arizona's worst desperados, the lawmen who brought them to justice, and how Fate changed their lives. Gathered by *Arizona Highways* from more than 70 years of writing about the Old West. Softcover. 144 pages.
#ADAP6 **$7.95**

Law Of The Gun
Historian and author Marshall Trimble presents an overview of those who wielded the gun to break the law, those who embraced the gun to uphold it, and the guns they used. You'll marvel at the stories of such compelling figures as Wyatt Earp, Wild Bill Hickok, John Wesley Hardin, Jesse James, the Daltons, and Judge Roy Bean. Includes 20 historic photos. Softcover. 192 pages.
#AGNP7 **$8.95**

They Left Their Mark: Heroes and Rogues of Arizona History
These larger-than-life characters have boldly written their names on the pages of Arizona history. From the early Spanish explorer Juan Bautista de Anza to land swindler James Addison Reavis to World War II Marine hero Ira Hayes, *They Left Their Mark* presents fascinating biographies of Arizona's famous and infamous. Softcover. 144 pages.
#ATMP7 **$7.95**

"MISSING ONE OF HIS CLASSES IS LIKE MISSING SOMETHING I'VE BOUGHT TICKETS FOR."

Bill Justice
Former College Student

"(HE'S) THE CHAMBER OF COMMERCE OF ARIZONA."

Arizona Republic

" ... HAS MORE STORIES TO TELL THEN THERE'S TIME FOR TELLING."

Scottsdale Progress-Tribune

" ... IS THE WILL ROGERS OF ARIZONA."

Pat McMahan
KTAR Radio

"ARIZONA'S COLORFUL HISTORY IS ALIVE AND WELL WITH MARSHALL TRIMBLE."

Barry Goldwater

" I THOUGHT I HAD THE BEST JOB IN THE WORLD — UNTIL I MET MARSHALL TRIMBLE."

Herb Drinkwater
Former Scottsdale Mayor